Ask your fellow cadets to sign your yearbook, then save it as a keepsake for the future

ARMY CADET YEARBOOK

ARMY CADET YEARBOOK

Editor: Jo Rees

Design: Dale Stiling

Copy: Kathryn Lewis, Abi Manning,
Rosanna Rothery, Selena Young

Production: Tamsin Powell

Commercial: Mark Tibbles

www.armycadets.com

ISBN 978-1-9160859-3-0

First published in Great Britain in 2020 by Army Cadet Force

Text © 2020 Army Cadet Force

Design and layout © 2020 Army Cadet Force

Printed in Great Britain

www.saltmedia.co.uk

01271 859299 ideas@saltmedia.co.uk

MIX
Paper from
responsible sources
FSC® C010353

ARMY CADET
YEARBOOK
Issue 1

Welcome

I'm very proud to introduce the first annual edition of the Army Cadet Yearbook. If ever there was a year in recent history that required recording for posterity, 2020 is surely it.

Dealing with the Covid-19 pandemic has been challenging on many fronts, yet both cadets and Cadet Force adult volunteers have shown fortitude, creativity and resolve in adapting to the cessation of face-to-face training and embracing the virtual space. You have all played your part in "keeping the flame alive". Thank you.

This Yearbook captures many fantastic examples of such activity. From cadets making PPE to those helping at hospitals and in the community – and let us not forget the cadet living in an Anderson shelter – each one exemplifies Army Cadets values.

In order for these stories to be remembered in years to come, we're printing (in addition to the softback-style book you're reading) a small number of cloth-bound print copies which will be made to last 100 years or longer in the Army Cadets' archive and the British Library. Future generations will read about how Army Cadets coped during this significant time.

As you delve into the book, you'll find it covers October 2019 to October 2020 and reveals activity that took place across the detachments and contingents during each month. This period began with the announcement of Lorraine Kelly as our National Honorary Colonel, followed by the first Army Cadet Force Conference with the incredible Jordan Wylie as our keynote speaker. Then there was lockdown which provided the ultimate opportunity for us to embrace our motto 'To Inspire To Achieve' in the face of enormous adversity. We draw the year to a close with the huge positive of the return to face-to-face training.

Read on to discover what individuals and detachments got up to during the year, meet inspiring adventurers and leaders, and discover more about the lives of the cadets. You'll also find lots of features which build on the life skills and opportunities we provide that set up young people for lifelong success.

We are the Army Cadets and this is our Yearbook.

Brigadier Stuart Williams OBE
Deputy Commander Cadets

Contents

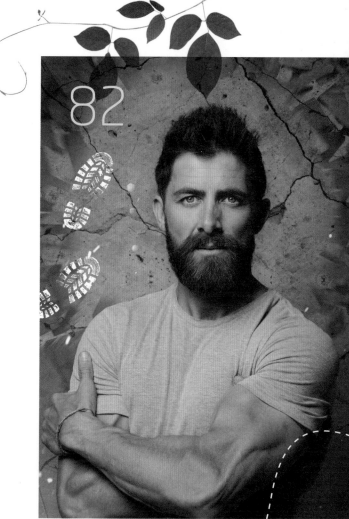

To Inspire To Achieve

Contents

126

204

166

Army Cadet life

OUR MOTTO To Inspire To Achieve

OUR VALUES

» COURAGE

Courage is both physical and moral. Physical courage is what lets us motivate others when the activity or the environment is hard or demanding, such as hiking across Dartmoor as part of a Ten Tors team. Moral courage is having the strength and confidence to do what is right even when it might make us unpopular, such as standing up to bullying. It is also the courage to insist on maintaining the highest standards of behaviour. Both physical and moral courage are equally important, and showing courage in all forms earns us respect and fosters trust.

» DISCIPLINE

Discipline helps us all to work as part of a team effectively. It isn't just about being told off for doing something wrong; it's about having the self-control to not do the wrong thing, and self-confidence to stand up to those who do.

Self-discipline is the ability to make the time to polish our boots, iron our uniform and be smart on parade, no matter what other distractions are around us.

Discipline helps build our team so everyone is trusted to do the task well. Good discipline means we all do the right thing – even when things get difficult.

» RESPECT FOR OTHERS

Respect for others means we treat others as we'd like to be treated.

Army Cadets is a very varied and mixed team, and we must not discriminate against anyone because they are male or female, or have a different ethnic background, religion or sexual orientation to us.

We recognise the value everyone brings to the team and that they all have different viewpoints and ways to contribute. We have respect for others, not only because it is a legal obligation, but because teams that embrace difference and diversity are stronger.

» LOYALTY

Loyalty is what keeps teams together. In the Army Cadets that team could be our detachment, our county, our section, our contingent or any other team we are part of, such as on an expedition, overseas exchange or sports team. When we work together in a team we achieve so much more. But loyalty must only support positive behaviours and actions – loyalty to a team should never allow poor behaviours or the wrong thing to be done. Letting others stray from our values is not loyal to the team.

© Daniel Turner Photography

» INTEGRITY

Integrity means being truthful and honest, and trusting those above us in the organisation.

When we show integrity we build trust in ourselves and in our team, and this makes the team stronger and able to do more. Showing integrity also helps others outside the Army Cadets trust us and helps us to do more in our communities. It is important that everyone, from the newest cadet to senior officers, demonstrates integrity in everything they do, otherwise trust will be eroded.

» SELFLESS COMMITMENT

Selfless commitment is critical to good leadership and teamwork. It is about putting the needs of others ahead of our own to help everyone succeed.

We demonstrate this when we help someone with a lesson they are finding difficult, rather than going off for a break, or when we hang back with someone who is struggling on an expedition, rather than speeding off ahead. Without selfless commitment we can't be good leaders. Remember, the motto of Royal Military Academy Sandhurst, where Army officers are trained, is 'Serve to Lead'.

© Carl Recine

Our charter

The Army Cadet Force is a national voluntary youth organisation. It is sponsored by the Army and provides challenging military, adventurous and community activities.

Its aim is to inspire young people to achieve success in life with a spirit of service to the Queen, their country and their local community, and to develop in them the qualities of good citizens. This is achieved by

❯ Providing progressive cadet training, often of a challenging and exciting nature, to foster confidence, self-reliance, initiative, loyalty and a sense of service to other people.

❯ Encouraging the development of personal powers of practical leadership and the ability to work successfully as a member of a team.

❯ Stimulating an interest in the Army, its achievements, skills and values.

❯ Advising and preparing those considering a career in the Services, or with the Reserve Forces.

Lorraine Kelly

At the start of lockdown we talked to Lorraine about what it was like to be (unexpectedly) presented with her Army Cadet title on live TV, her thoughts about the movement, and her thwarted ambition.

No one who watched Lorraine on her special 60th birthday TV programme could have failed to tear up at the genuine emotion she displayed when asked if she'd take on the role of being the Army Cadet Force's new National Honorary Colonel.

'Seriously?' she asked with huge surprise, followed by a tearful: *'Gosh. I am so honoured, I really am.'*

What are her memories of that morning?

'I was so emotional. They did it live on the show and, of all the things that went on that morning, that was the one that touched me most. It was a massive, massive honour.

'I feel that part of my job now is being an ambassador for the cadet movement and letting everyone know how fantastic the volunteers are. We wouldn't have the movement if it wasn't for them giving their time, energy, enthusiasm and passion: they're astonishing.'

And the cadets? *'I would love every single young person in the country to have the opportunity, should they choose, to be a cadet as it would give them a lot of confidence.'*

A long-time supporter of the armed forces (she's also an ambassador for Help for Heroes), Lorraine's formal relationship with Army Cadets started in 2009 when she was made Honorary Colonel of the Black Watch Battalion ACF in Scotland. She says: *'I loved doing that. Like a lot of people, I had never realised what amazing work was being done, so it was wonderful for me to get that opportunity in Scotland. What I really noticed was that while not everyone who joins the Cadets goes on to be in the Armed Forces, everyone who joins will be a better person for it – and better at whatever they go on to do in life.*

'I love the friendships made and the sense of togetherness, which is exactly what we need at the moment. All the ways we are told we should live our lives are the values that are essential to the Cadet experience: being the best you can be, showing community spirit, being generous, being kind. They're all values that cadets have and hopefully, when this is over, the world will be more like the Cadet movement.'

She also sees teamwork as a key cadet quality: *'You're only as good as the weakest link in your chain, so it's important to make sure everyone gets the help they need. Everyone has different skills: maybe you're academic but you can't put a plug on, but your pal can, or maybe someone else has good leadership skills. When you pool those skills together it's powerful.'*

What does she think Army Cadets gives young people in terms of qualities, skills and values?

'It's being a more caring and considerate person who thinks about others, and about developing self confidence,' she says. 'Those skills set you up for life, no matter what you decide to do.

'It's also about community – and that's never been more important. It's about thinking about others and helping others, maybe in a practical way. It doesn't have to be huge: it could be going to get someone the paper or checking in on them. Putting others first is important – if we all did that, what an amazing world it would be.'

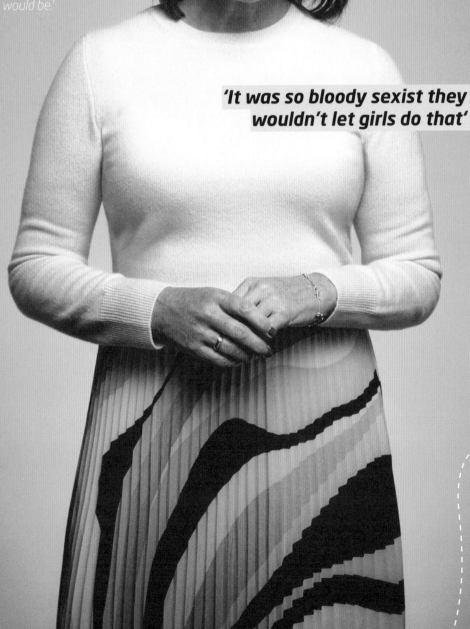

'It was so bloody sexist they wouldn't let girls do that'

Did she have an opportunity to develop those kinds of skills when she was young?

'I was in the Brownies and the Girl Guides and, of course, it's not exactly the same (and back then it was quite different to how it is now) but anything that requires you to be part of a group is great.

'Cutbacks have meant we don't have so many youth clubs nowadays and Army Cadets fills that gap. Anything that takes you away from being self-absorbed and makes you part of a team is helpful.'

'It was a massive, massive honour'

What values does she live her life by?

'When I was a kid I was taught "do as you would be done by". That sounds very old fashioned but we were taught to help others and that we had a social responsibility, so that's certainly something I try to do.

'We all have to help in our own way. I've volunteered as an NHS Volunteer Responder and, while I'm not able to drive people around, I can listen if people want to talk on the phone.'

Despite doing what may seem to be a pretty glamorous day job, Lorraine is keen to emphasise that her life off-camera is somewhat different: *'As soon as I come off air, it's on with the jeans and trainers,'* she laughs. *'I'm actually a pretty adventurous person. I went to Antarctica a few years back and followed in the footsteps of Ernest Shackleton which was incredible. I even did a polar dip – crazy, but it had to be done.*

'I like a challenge: I've done four marathons – three London, one New York. I also did a 100-mile trudge through the desert in Kenya for charity, which was very tough but an amazing experience.'

If she'd been born a little later her career might have been very different, as her girlhood ambition was to be a pilot in the RAF. However, she says: *'Back then it was so bloody sexist*

they wouldn't let girls do that. I wasn't able to fulfil my ambition to be a pilot, but, because of my job, I've been up in a couple of jets – including a Tornado, which was amazing.

'It's never been easier for girls than it is now – we've come so far. And the same goes for people who are gay or trans – and it's brilliant to see. I'm so encouraged by the number of young women who are in the Cadets.'

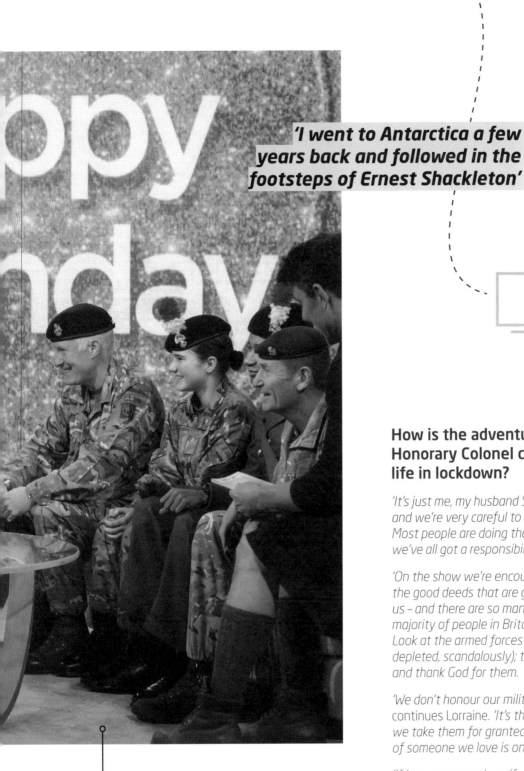

'I went to Antarctica a few years back and followed in the footsteps of Ernest Shackleton'

Lorraine with cadets and Brigadier Stuart Williams OBE, Brigadier Mark Christie OBE and presenter Ben Shephard on her TV show when awarded the title of National Honorary Colonel of the Army Cadet Force.

How is the adventurous National Honorary Colonel coping with life in lockdown?

'It's just me, my husband Steve and our wee dog and we're very careful to be apart from everyone. Most people are doing that, but not everyone, yet we've all got a responsibility.

'On the show we're encouraging people to share the good deeds that are going on all around us – and there are so many of them. The vast majority of people in Britain are doing their bit. Look at the armed forces (as much as they are depleted, scandalously); they are all helping out and thank God for them.

'We don't honour our military personnel enough,' continues Lorraine. *'It's the same with the NHS: we take them for granted until our life or the life of someone we love is on the line.*

'If I see someone in uniform I always make a point of thanking them for their service. I know it's very American but I think it's important. One thing that I think will come out of this experience is that we won't take the NHS, Armed Forces, other first responders or those brilliant people who empty the bins for granted again. They are literally putting their life on the line. It's very humbling.'

Meet our
AMBASSADORS

In 2019 we launched the Army Cadet Ambassador and Champion programme. Here's what you need to know about our amazing supporters ...

Jordan Wylie

Army Cadets Ambassador Jordan is a former soldier, bestselling author, extreme adventurer and one of the stars of Channel 4's BAFTA-nominated shows *Hunted* and *Celebrity Hunted*.

He served for a decade in the British Army where he specialised in military intelligence, reconnaissance and surveillance operations.

'Jordan is one of the stars of Channel 4's BAFTA-nominated shows Hunted and Celebrity Hunted'

On leaving the Army, Jordan entered the world of maritime security, making headlines when a ship he was protecting was attacked by armed Somali pirates. This experience led to the writing of his 2017 bestseller *Citadel: The True Story of One Man's War Against the Pirates of Somalia.*

He's undertaken numerous major charity expeditions including Running Dangerously and Barefoot Warrior which involved climbing Mount Kilimanjaro barefoot.

Jordan has battled with severe depression, chronic anxiety and epilepsy, and campaigns to reduce the stigma around mental illness.

Of his involvement with Army Cadets he says: *'It's an amazing youth organisation that inspires boys and girls to develop themselves, enjoy fun activities and build friendships in a safe, positive and inclusive environment. When a cadet puts on their uniform they are part of a big team – no matter what their background.'*

Read more about Jordan's involvement in our Guinness World Records™ attempt on page 190.

To Inspire To Achieve

Craig Mathieson

Polar explorer Craig has many years of military and mountaineering experience and been involved in numerous expeditions to the Antarctic and Arctic.

He led the first dedicated Scottish expedition to the South Pole in 2004; skied to the North Pole in 2006; was appointed Explorer-in-Residence by Royal Scottish Geographical Society in 2013; and recently became membership director of the Great Britain and Ireland Chapter of The Explorers Club.

Craig also runs The Polar Academy, a project that takes young people in Scotland on challenging and confidence-building expeditions to the Arctic.

The Academy's motto is 'Inspiration through Exploration' and it identifies 'invisible' secondary school children between the ages of 14 and 17 who are crushed by a lack of self-esteem, and gives them the chance to redefine their physical and mental limits.

Participants are put through a rigorous ten-month training programme before being immersed in the wilds of Greenland, navigating through some of the world's remotest terrain for ten days.

'Taking young people on challenging expeditions to the Arctic'

On their return to Scotland, each pupil shares their experiences with their peer group, speaking to more than 20,000 school children in their region. They're living proof that ordinary pupils can achieve the truly extraordinary.

On his involvement with Army Cadets, Craig says: *'It offers young people an opportunity to enjoy exciting activities in a safe and inclusive environment, something I feel very passionate about.'*

Sally Orange

Army Cadets Ambassador Sally is an endurance runner, adventurer, mental health champion and multiple Guinness World Records™ title holder.

In addition to having run over 50 marathons in every continent of the world – including the gruelling Marathon des Sables – Sally had a distinguished 22-year military career in the Royal Army Medical Corps as a physiotherapy officer.

She also captained the first British female team to complete the world's toughest cycle race – the Race Across America – and has cycled the length of New Zealand, swum the English Channel relay, completed eight Ironman triathlons, climbed numerous 6,000m+ mountains, and skied 250km across the largest plateau in the Arctic Circle, raising thousands of pounds for charity.

'Sally has run over 50 marathons - including the gruelling Marathon des Sables'

Sally has publicly shared her experience of suffering from severe depression and chronic anxiety and is committed to raising awareness to help others.

Read more about Sally's involvement in our Guinness World Records™ attempt on page 190.

'Big Phil' Campion

Army Cadets Champion Phil is a former soldier, author and TV personality.

Phil had a challenging start in life: he was given up for adoption at birth and subsequently sent to a series of children's homes. However, he found his natural environment as a member of the CCF at school, and left formal education aged 16 to join the Royal Hampshire Regiment.

Phil passed his Commando course, P Company and Special Forces selection, and his career took him on operational service to Northern Ireland, West Africa and the Balkans, among other parts of the world.

'Phil's first book Born Fearless became a Sunday Times bestseller'

In 2011, he wrote his first book (he's published four) *Born Fearless* which became a *Sunday Times* bestseller. He also starred in his own TV documentary *Big Phil's War* for Sky.

Since leaving the military, Phil has helped raise the profile and funds of numerous charities and good causes. In 2005 he invented the UTag, a USB stick contained in a dog tag, which holds the wearer's ID, and medical and contact details.

Phil's stated aim in life has been to put in as much as he's taken out, and being Champion of the ACF has given him an opportunity to achieve this.

Army Cadets in
October 2019

British Citizen Youth Awards for two cadets

The British Citizen Youth Award recognises young people who have done extraordinary things for the good of their country, so it was fantastic to see two cadets presented with honours in October.

Cadet Sergeant Major Ben Harbottle, 16, of Durham ACF and **Cadet Amy Barbour**, 16, of West Lowland Bn ACF attended the formal presentation at the Palace of Westminster with family, friends and Deputy Commander Cadets Brigadier Stuart Williams OBE (who attended as a guest of Cadet Barbour).

Ben was unable to speak properly until he was nine years old, and spent his early years being ignored or bullied. As a result, his academic performance was poor. However, undeterred by his school environment, he set himself the challenge of passing his GCSEs with good grades and, as a result of his hard work, surpassed all expectations.

It was during this period that Ben joined Durham ACF. His cadet career has seen him take part in an exchange to Canada, become a 4 Star Staff Sergeant Major, pass his Master Cadet course and be appointed Lord Lieutenant's Cadet for Tyne and Wear 2019.

His journey is a testament to his determination, and his ambition now is to become an Army officer. Ben said: '*I was determined not to let my speech and educational difficulties stop me achieving my goals, but the Army Cadet Force inspired me to aim even higher. My motto is "attitude determines altitude".*'

Amy has been a young carer since the age of five but, despite the pressure of this responsibility, she has studied tirelessly at school to achieve A grades and become an integral member of her ACF detachment.

Amy said: '*Given the common misconception that young people are unmotivated troublemakers, it was incredibly encouraging and inspiring to see the achievements of so many of my peers [at the awards]. I am extremely proud to have the award ... however, I am even more grateful to my battalion for their unfaltering support.*'

Amy took her Highers early and aims to become an Army doctor.

To Inspire To Achieve

© Ben Stevens

STEM camp takes place

The fourth annual STEM (Science, Technology, Engineering and Mathematics) camp took place on Salisbury Plain from 26 October to 1 November.

The camp was an opportunity for cadets aged 12-16 to get exciting hands-on experience and learn from the Army's leading STEM experts.

In addition to speaking to officers and Army soldiers about how STEM is integrated into their roles, and taking a look at some of the kit and equipment used, cadets got to take part in the following sessions:

- Army Air Corps (AAC) explaining rotary wing (helicopter) flight.

- Adjutant General's Corps (AGC) – which provides teachers, lawyers and accountants to the Army – revealed how it uses hi-tech forensic techniques to solve cases.

- Army Medical Services (AMS) – which includes medics, vets, dentists and nurses – demonstrated how the Army looks after its personnel and animals.

- Royal Artillery (RA) talked about the use of unmanned aerial vehicles (UAVs) for battlefield surveillance and information-gathering, along with a practical session operating drones.

- Royal Electrical and Mechanical Engineers (REME) showed how modern equipment is recovered and repaired.

- Royal Logistic Corps (RLC) explained how the Army is sustained in the field, including munitions, fuels and an explosives demonstration.

- Royal Signals demonstrated a range of state-of-the-art military communications equipment and the latest cybersecurity initiatives.

Cadets march for General Sir Nick Carter

A group of year 8 and 9 cadets from the Mossbourne Federation CCF (London Borough of Hackney) performed their inaugural parade and inspection for the Chief of the Defence Staff General Sir Nick Carter, GCB, CBE, DSO, ADC.

They marched with The Band of the Coldstream Guards to mark the Federation's initiation into the national Cadet Expansion Programme.

Western Isles cadets meet the Princess Royal

Cadet Lance Corporal Aiden Jamieson (14) and Cadet Heidi MacLeod (12) of 1st Battalion The Highlanders' West Lewis Detachment welcomed the Princess Royal on her visit to the Flannan Isles Memorial and Exhibition.

The memorial remembers Flannan Isles lighthouse keepers James Ducat, Thomas Marshall and Donald MacArthur who vanished from the lighthouse in 1900, a mystery that has intrigued for over a century.

ADVENTURERS

Read on to discover what happened when Captain
Louis Rudd MBE attempted a 920-mile solo trek
across Antarctica; find out what Colonel (Retd)
David Radford-Wilson MBE learnt from taking part
in the Army Mount Everest West Ridge Expedition;
and take a look at Army Cadet Adventurous Training.

Louis Rudd on his 56-day
solo trek across Antarctica

'You are living above the
clouds and get to watch
the world come sparkling
into life each day'

What I learnt ...
CLIMBING EVEREST

Colonel (Retd) David Radford-Wilson MBE
was a leader of the Army Mount Everest West Ridge Expedition, which aimed to reach the top of the mountain via the West Ridge. It's an ascent previously completed by just four people – and where more climbers have died than succeeded.

If you want something amazing, you have to work hard to make it happen. I got a call one day from one of the other leaders who asked if I fancied going climbing. He explained that he had the idea of undertaking the first ever British ascent of the West Ridge of Everest and doing it as a tri-service military expedition.

Of course I agreed, but it then took three years to achieve: planning; building a big squad so that as many people as possible could be part of the journey; training; buying the equipment and raising the money to do it – and that was before we even got to China (where we then spent three months on the mountain).

To do amazing things, you have to build amazing teams. Pulling together a tight-knit group of like-minded souls who want to do the same thing leads to results – and a lot of fun.

We had to work extremely well together, climbing up each section while carrying equipment, before coming down again to sleep. You do that again and again until,

eventually, you are camped as high as possible while you wait for the window (which could be mere days) that occurs twice a year when the jet stream rises above Everest. That's your opportunity to climb to the top and down again.

'We climbed the equivalent height of Everest seven times'

I calculated that, as a result of carrying all the tents and equipment up, we climbed the equivalent height of Everest seven times.

Our bodies and minds are so much more capable than we believe. It's only by challenging ourselves do we learn that something that seems impossible can be done.

You can feel humbled and empowered at the same time. The north face fills you with emotion. I felt privileged to be there and excited – but also fearful. The first time I went on the mountain it was late in the afternoon

and getting dark; it was a very frightening place to be and I only wanted to get off there. Then, being on the mountain again the next day in the sun was so uplifting. You feel so insignificant, yet it's amazingly powerful to be at one with that massive, powerful environment.

A good night's sleep and a conversation with a friend quells doubts and fears. At times you doubt whether you are good enough or if you can do it; everyone who finds themselves in a big adventure feels that. The mental challenges are harder than the physical ones, especially for the junior members who, although very fit and strong, may not have had their minds tested in this way before. Food, sleep and an honest chat all help you cope better.

Everest is incredibly beautiful – from the tiniest ice crystals to watching the sun fire off laser-like beams of light from the mountain peaks first thing in the morning. You are living above the clouds and get to watch the world come sparkling into life each day.

You must be prepared to fail. No experienced mountaineer has reached the top of as many mountains as they've climbed. In the end, the main team had to turn back just 600 metres from the summit because there was too much soft snow on the north face and the avalanche risk was just too great.

We didn't succeed in our mission, but so many positives came out of it and we had such a life-changing experience that we wouldn't have changed it for the world.

I wouldn't have been able to do it unless it was in a military expedition. Civilian expeditions are very different – you're with strangers so there's no bond and you're using equipment you've never seen before, being rushed up and down a tourist trail.

Camping with the Cadets ultimately led me to Everest. Those teenage camping trips were my first experience of being scared and exhilarated in a tent on a hillside. Being in the Cadets led me into climbing and mountaineering, and one of the reasons I joined the Army was because I loved being outdoors and doing adventurous training.

'Being in the Cadets led me into climbing and mountaineering'

At the time of the
expedition – which became
the most successful high-
altitude military expedition the
Army has ever run – David had just
finished commanding a Special Forces
squadron. He retired from the Army
after 25 years' service and now
runs a disaster response and
relief company which works
all over the world.

Louis was the second person (by a matter of hours) to achieve the feat of solo-trekking across Antarctica unassisted, and the first (and only) to have traversed it twice on foot.

Spirit of
ENDURANCE

In 2019 **Captain Louis Rudd MBE** completed a 920-mile solo trek across Antarctica in an attempt to do it before anyone else. He reveals the highs and the lows of his astonishing adventure.

Very few people in the history of humankind have experienced what it's like to haul a sledge – alone – through Antarctica for 56 days.

Captain Louis Rudd turned 50 as he completed this adventure in January 2019. It was an unusual way to celebrate a big birthday and was to be his last major expedition as a serving Army officer.

During his 35-year career as a Royal Marine commando and SAS soldier Louis completed tours of duty in Kosovo and Afghanistan, as well as taking part in incredible adventurous training around the world.

On retirement, he wrote a book called *Endurance* which tells the story of the expedition. In 2019 Louis was named the Scientific Exploration Society's Explorer of the Year.

When did your interest in adventurous expeditions begin?

'I wasn't particularly academic as a youngster, but I was outdoorsy and always looking for adventure.

'At school I wasn't the best behaved and when I was 12 my mate and I had an altercation with a maths

teacher. We were sent to the headmaster for a caning; my mate went in first and I sat in the waiting area outside, feeling pretty terrified.

'Aged 14 I was determined to have an adventure and cycled from Lincolnshire to my dad's farm in Scotland'

'While I was waiting for my turn, I picked up a book at random from the shelf: it was a Ladybird book called Captain Scott. I'd never heard of Scott of the Antarctic or his epic struggle to reach the South Pole – and it blew my mind. It was at that point that I thought, *I want to be a polar explorer.*

'I read on and discovered that Scott's men had perished on their journey and, all of a sudden, getting caned didn't seem such a big deal.

'After that I read everything I could about Scott and Shackleton and, at the start of my summer holidays when I was 14, I read a book about Ranulph Fiennes. He inspired me because he was both a living and a British polar adventurer.

'My dad was working as a commercial diver on the oil rigs off Aberdeen at the time and, after reading the Fiennes book, I was determined to have an adventure myself and decided to cycle from Lincolnshire to my dad's farm in Scotland.

'My mum told me not to be ridiculous as I only had a basic kid's bike with three gears and no lights, but I hatched a plan. I told her I was going out for a cycle the next day and set off at 6am with a road map, a bit of pocket money I'd saved up, a puncture repair kit and a basic sleeping bag.

'After I'd ridden a hundred miles I phoned my mum from a call box and told her where I was heading. Of course she went ballistic, but there was nothing she could do. I cycled via the back routes until about 11pm each evening and then crashed in my sleeping bag in a field at the side of the road. Then I'd get up at first light and carry on. After five and a half days – 550 miles – I got to my dad's. That was my first expedition.'

Were you an Army Cadet?

'I was an Air Cadet. There were no Army Cadet detachments near where I lived in Lincolnshire.

'From a young age I was interested in joining the Marines and I thought that being in the Cadets (wearing uniform and learning the terminology) would prepare me for that. I joined the Marines straight out of school, aged 16, and it was quite a culture shock.'

What drives you to put yourself through long and arduous expeditions?

'There are multiple reasons behind all of my trips. Firstly, I'm interested in doing something that hasn't been done before. Secondly, I always fundraise for a good cause – I'm an ambassador for ABF The Soldiers' Charity.

'On a couple of the trips, I've also been a guinea pig for medical research into weight loss in cancer patients. Then there is the love of Antarctica as a place: I'm fascinated by the raw beauty of the pristine environment which is untouched by mankind. And, finally, I'm a big fan of the history of polar exploration.'

What small comforts did you miss while you were on your recent expedition?

'Fresh food: the bulk of your 24-hour ration is freeze dried to save weight (you reconstitute it with melted snow) and while you also have a snack bag of frozen pieces of chocolate and salami, it's tasteless when it's super cold. Because I was losing body fat, I dreamt of steak and chips and full English breakfasts.'

How difficult did you find being completely alone for two months?

'It wasn't really an issue. Thirty-five years of military service helped me build mental resilience which is essential on extreme expeditions. Also, repeatedly going through the process of leaving home to go on tour to places like Afghanistan, and then having to transition back into family life, was a sort of rehearsal for the trips to Antarctica.

'One of the weirdest things was when, after spending those two months alone, I was dropped off in Chile and then headed straight to New York for media interviews. It was teeming with people and I was bombarded

the ultimate selfie

with questions on multiple chat shows. I was quite overwhelmed at times and had to keep taking myself off for five minutes.'

What kind of psychological coping strategies did you use during the expedition?

'Before I went, I worked with a psychologist friend and we came up with some strategies which really helped me. One was breaking the whole trip down into ten-day blocks, at the end of which I would reward myself with a freeze-dried chocolate pudding. I'd fixate on getting to the end of the block of ten days as it was less daunting than thinking about the entire trip in one go.

'I'd also written down in my diary and on the inside of the tent why I was doing the trip. I was raising money for people who had lost limbs and who would have a lifetime of challenges ahead so, on days when I felt a bit sorry for myself, I remembered that and that I had chosen to be there – and that it would come to an end.

'I also found audiobooks very helpful – I had about 60 stored on my phone. If it was a bad day with howling winds and no visibility, I found it comforting to have a human voice in my headphones and would pretend there was someone skiing alongside me, narrating the story.

'It was comforting to have a human voice in my headphones'

'When I took my first trip to Antarctica in 2011 I made so many mistakes psychologically: I fought against the environment and the conditions and, if I had a bad day, I'd have a hissy fit and throw my ski poles around.

'I've completely changed and now accept what I can't control and only worry about things I can change. If I'd tried to do the solo trip with my mindset as it was in 2011 I think I'd have completely lost the plot.'

What advice would you give your teenage self?

'If you've got a dream, no matter how insurmountable it might look, you can make things happen if you are determined and take action. Begin with small steps and, as long as you're moving forward, you'll eventually get somewhere.'

'I'm fascinated by the raw beauty of the pristine environment which is untouched by mankind'

"Onwards"

Cadets Adventurous Training

To Inspire To Achieve

In 2020, Adventurous Training was made an essential part of the cadet syllabus for the first time. National Adviser **Cath Davies** gives us the lowdown.

'There's growing evidence that time spent in the outdoors is great for mental as well as physical health'

What is Adventurous Training (AT)?

'AT encompasses a wide range of outdoor activities which are designed to teach both 'hard' skills (the practical techniques required to participate in an activity) and 'soft' skills (the personal development gained from such experiences).'

What key skills can cadets expect to learn?

'While cadets will learn practical skills such as navigation, understanding weather forecasts and campcraft, they'll also develop mental and physical robustness, resilience, self-reliance, initiative, confidence, teamwork, risk management and leadership.

'All of these attributes are transferable skills which cadets can use in both their other cadet activities and in their academic lives. They're skills for life which they may even use in their future careers.'

What are the benefits?

'AT exposes cadets to environments they may not otherwise get to experience, both in the UK and abroad. Travel to remote areas overseas can enable cadets to experience other cultures and gain a greater understanding of the diversity of humankind.

'There's growing evidence, too, that time spent in the outdoors is great for mental and physical health.'

The Ulysses Trust

The Ulysses Trust provides grants for reservist and cadet AT expeditions and in 2019 supported 11 Army Cadet expeditions, enabling 217 cadets and 74 CFAVs to participate. Check out some of the most exciting recent trips.

Kayaking in northern Norway

The Cadet Centre for Adventurous Training took its entire fleet of sea kayaks to the Lofoten Islands in August 2019. Nine cadets, three CFAVs and two instructors paddled a total of 122km through northern Norway.

The group built up their skills and confidence during the first half of the exercise, so they were well prepared for the three-day 80km remote wilderness expedition that followed.

'Travel to remote areas overseas enables cadets to experience other cultures'

Alpine trekking in Germany

In July 2019, eight cadets and four CFAVs from Gloucestershire ACF deployed to Garmisch, Germany to learn about Alpine trekking and elementary mountaineering in a challenging environment.

They undertook several gruelling treks in a variety of weather conditions and donned crampons to traverse the Kodnitzkees Glacier. The experience was a physical and mental challenge for all of the participants.

South African battlefields tour

Warwickshire and West Midlands ACF deployed to South Africa in August 2019. The expedition involved educational battlefield tours of Rorke's Drift, conservation activities and engagement with a local orphanage.

Although the expedition was primarily a community engagement tour, all travelling to locations was done on foot, with the cadets carrying small rucksacks in expedition conditions, while support vehicles took the bulk of the kit. In total they walked 70km over ten days in very difficult undulating terrain.

GO » FURTHER

Interested in putting together an Adventurous Training expedition? Contact The Ulysses Trust via its website as it welcomes applications from cadet units across the UK – especially those that support disadvantaged young people.

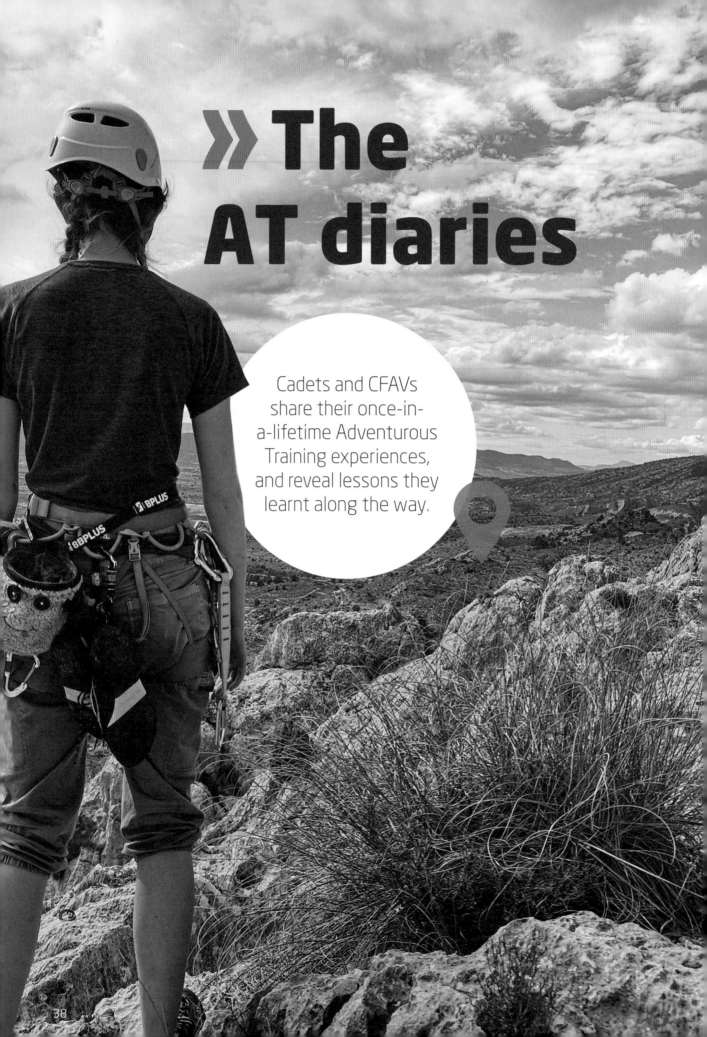

» The AT diaries

Cadets and CFAVs share their once-in-a-lifetime Adventurous Training experiences, and reveal lessons they learnt along the way.

'My heart was pounding but it was actually absolutely thrilling'

Cadet Rock, Calpe, Spain

Abigail Robertson, 2nd Lieutenant, Stanley Detachment, Black Watch Battalion

'The Cadet Rock trip is an advanced course for rock climbers who've already passed their basic training, and the aim of the training was to do multi-pitching on the sports routes for which Calpe is known.

'On the first day we were put into pairs and assigned an instructor who took us out to assess our levels of experience. Then, each day after that, we kept developing our skills and technique. So, from the get-go, we were pushing the boundaries.

'I remember the first time we did a multi-pitch: our instructor was climbing above us and my partner (a cadet) and I were sat on a tiny ledge above a huge cliff. We turned to each other, petrified – but not scared to the point that we wanted to get

off the mountain. My heart was pounding but it was actually absolutely thrilling.

'We moved onto lead climbing which made it a great course for developing trust with a climbing partner. You have to have complete faith they're going to catch you when you fall – and that also greatly improves your communication with each other.

'I'd encourage cadets and CFAVs to go on AT trips whenever they can as there are so many benefits: it develops your confidence, gets you out of your comfort zone in a safe environment (all of the instructors are very knowledgeable), and improves teamwork – among so many other skills. You walk away with new skills and new friends.'

'It was incredible: there was no one else around, just our small group surrounded by snow and mountains'

Cadet Canski Ski F2, Banff, Canada

Emma Mackenzie, Stanley Detachment, Black Watch Battalion

'A group of ten of us went to Banff in the Rockies for six days at the start of 2020. I've skied quite a lot before (twice with the ACF) but this trip was great because everyone in the group was at a similar level.

'The first two days were spent skiing with our two instructors in the resorts. On days three and four we got a bus to the middle of nowhere and completed a touring course. We had skins on our skis and walked up the mountain in them before skiing back down. It was my first time touring and it was incredible: there was no one else around, just our small group surrounded by snow and mountains.

'In our final few days, we received avalanche training – you don't get many opportunities to learn skills like those in situ.

'The best thing about the trip was going to Canada, which is so different from skiing in Europe: it's a lot higher than the Alps and it's definitely harder.

'A great thing about AT trips is that you mix with new people from different parts of the UK, unlike at camps where you're with your detachment. I'm still in touch with the group from the ski trip.'

GR20 Hiking, Corsica, France

Charlotte Taylor, 2nd Lieutenant, Staffordshire and West Midlands ACF

'I was 17 and one of the senior cadets when I went on the two-week expedition to Corsica to complete the GR20 – Europe's hardest hiking route.

'We went in summer so the first two days were spent acclimatising to the hot weather and getting supplies. We started the trek in Calvi and spent three days going across the mountains following rocks with red and white markings, and staying in campsites close to the trail. Every three days we'd meet up with the instructors who were trailing us in a support car to stock up the food supplies and check our route.

'The trek was really tough: it was hot, there were steep mountains to climb, and within the group of 16 we had a range of different physical abilities. Even the rest days were spent walking, so it was also mentally challenging – some days I thought, *Is this ever going to end?* We had to draw on great mental strength to keep going and support the team.

'The last day of the walk was all downhill and the views were fantastic. When we got down we

looked back at this amazing mountain and had a huge sense of accomplishment. Just before the trip I'd lost my grandad, and when we finished I had a feeling that he'd have been so proud.'

'We looked back at this amazing mountain and had a huge sense of accomplishment'

'We were split into two teams, and although mine wasn't the first to finish we still had smiles on our faces at the end and a good laugh along the way – that's what it's about.'

Army Cadets in
November 2019

Senior Cadet Conference at CTC Frimley Park

Sixty-one cadets attended the Senior Cadet Conference which took place at CTC Frimley Park on 15-17 November, making it the biggest – and most successful – Senior Cadet Conference to date.

The annual event is an important date in the calendar for senior cadets, as it's their opportunity to help shape the future of the organisation by discussing ideas and suggesting strategies which may then by rolled out nationwide.

Guest speakers on the weekend included Lt Col Alijah RAPTC, Col Riley ACF (Regional Command ACF Colonel Cadets), Lt Col G Moncur MBE ACF, Army Sergeant Major WO1 G Patton and Field Army Sergeant Major WO1 P Carney.

Northumbria ACF

Lest we forget

Remembrance Sunday parades were held on 10 November, and cadets and CFAVs across the UK took part to honour and remember the servicemen and servicewomen who died in combat in the two World Wars and other conflicts.

Cadets played a huge role in organising events in the run-up to Remembrance Day, including helping maintain local war memorials, fundraising for the Poppy Appeal, organising band performances and working with the Royal British Legion.

During Remembrance Day, detachments turned out in force, marching and laying wreaths as part of the poignant commemorative ceremonies.

Army Cadet Force National Swimming Competition

On Saturday 23 November, swimmers from across the UK competed in the annual ACF National Swimming Competition, held at Hindley Leisure Centre in Liverpool.

Eastern Region 7 X Brigade took home the highly sought-after trophy and each team member was also awarded their own medal.

TAKE THE TEST

Would you know
what to do if you were
caught in a rip current,
found yourself in a kayak crisis,
had to deal with hypothermia
or heat exhaustion, or needed
to fend off wild predators?
Here's your chance
to find out ...

Rip current

Think you'd know what to do if you were caught in a rip current? Take the test and find out.

The scenario

You're on holiday and taking a dip in the ocean. You swim out to what looks like calm, clear water but, before long, you realise you're further from the shore than you intended.

You turn to swim back to the beach, only to find yourself at the mercy of a powerful, fast-moving current which is pulling you back out into the ocean. Should you ...

A

Use every bit of strength and stamina to swim back to shore. Work vigorously and go directly against the flow of the rip which will be intent on pushing you out to sea.

B

Swim parallel to the shore until free of the rip and then use breaking waves to help you reach the beach.

C

Stay in the calmer water and avoid the rougher looking white water at all costs. Use vigorous strokes to swim around and stay afloat until the rip current subsides.

Rips 101

❯ Rips are strong currents running out to sea, which can rapidly drag people away from the shallows and into deeper water. They're especially powerful in larger surf and can also be found around river mouths and estuaries.

Rips can be difficult to spot but are sometimes identified by a channel of churning, choppy water on the sea's surface or, conversely, seemingly calm stretches of water between crashing waves.

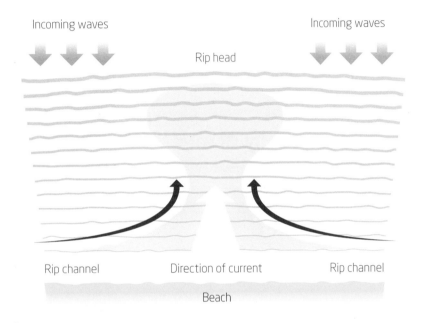

Incoming waves   Incoming waves

Rip head

Rip channel   Direction of current   Rip channel

Beach

Answer

(The answer is **B**)

First: *DON'T PANIC*

If you feel you're panicking, float (if possible on your back) and take a series of slow, calming breaths. If you have a surfboard or bodyboard, use this to help keep afloat.

If you are not a strong swimmer or find yourself struggling, don't hesitate to raise your arm and call for help (and even if you feel able to get out of the rip, it pays to have help).

Don't try to swim back to shore against the rip as you'll quickly become exhausted.

If you are able to stand, wade out of the current rather than swim (rips can flow at 4-5mph – faster than an Olympic swimmer).

If the water is too deep to stand in and you're a confident swimmer, swim across the direction of the current, parallel to the shore, until you are free.

Use any breaking waves to help you get back to the beach. If you don't feel confident to swim, raise your arm and float while waiting for help.

Rip currents don't go on forever and usually stop flowing out to sea soon after the furthest breaking waves.

Always stay between the red and yellow flags on lifeguarded beaches which indicate where to swim safely. If you spot anyone in trouble, alert the lifeguards or call 999 or 112 and ask for the coastguard.

Heat exhaustion

You're hiking with friends and one of them develops heat exhaustion. Would you know what to do? Army Cadet Ambassador **Sally Orange** reveals the best strategy.

The scenario

You're hiking with friends in high summer. It is warm when you set out in the morning, and by mid-afternoon you've covered a lot of ground and the temperature has soared.

One of your friends who isn't used to the heat starts to complain of a headache, feels dizzy and has cramp in their legs. They forgot their hat and are obviously feeling the effects of being exposed to the sun all day. You're concerned because they look pale and their skin is a bit clammy. Should you …

A
Give them your hat to wear and carry on, aiming to get home as soon as possible.

B
Encourage them to sit down immediately to rest for a couple of hours.

C
Find some shade and make them lie down with their feet raised. Give them plenty to drink.

To Inspire To Achieve

Heat exhaustion 101

❯ In hot weather, we mainly cool ourselves by sweating. However, when we exercise strenuously in hot and humid conditions, our bodies are less able to cool efficiently, which can lead to heat exhaustion. If untreated, this can develop further into heatstroke, which can be life threatening.

Signs of heat exhaustion include headache, dizziness, confusion, feeling sick, excessive sweating and pale, clammy skin. Other symptoms are cramps in the arms, legs and stomach (known as heat cramps), fast breathing or pulse rate, being very thirsty, and having a temperature of 38°c or above.

Answer

(The answer is **C**)

Heat exhaustion is caused by a loss of salt and water, usually through excessive sweating. It develops slowly and often happens to people who aren't used to hot, humid weather.

If someone is showing signs of heat exhaustion, they need to be cooled down quickly.

'The best way to do this is to move them into the shade where they can rest,' says Sally. *'Get them to lie down and raise their feet slightly – you could put them on a rucksack.*

'Give them plenty of water (or sports rehydration fluids to replace electrolytes) and cool their skin by sponging them with water. If you have a cloth or T-shirt, you can wet it and place on their forehead or the back of their neck, which will also help cool them down.

'Keep checking on their response; if their condition seems to be getting worse place them in the recovery position,' she explains.

Sally knows all there is to know about identifying heat exhaustion as she's completed (among a total of 54 marathons) the toughest footrace on Earth: the Marathon des Sables, where competitors cover 254km in 48°c heat over six days.

'It's so gruelling,' says Sally. *'At the end of my first day I was kept in the medical tent for an hour and a half as they were considering putting me on an intravenous drip to rehydrate me. I was suffering from being out in extreme temperatures for so many hours.*

'Preparation is key to avoiding heat exhaustion,' she adds. *'Avoid the sun between 11am–3pm when the temperatures are high and use*

the Met Office website or app to check the forecast when doing your planning. Always wear a wide-brimmed hat and light-coloured, loose clothing in hot weather, and take sun cream as well as plenty of fluids with you.

'If you have a friend who is suffering in the heat, think about what they are carrying and share the load among the group, stopping as soon as you can to rest in the shade and get them rehydrated and cooled down.'

If you can't get them cooled down within half an hour, call 999 and ask for help. Heat exhaustion can develop into heatstroke, which needs to be treated as an emergency.

Kayak crisis

Think you'd know what to do if you got blown out to sea while kayaking?

The scenario

It's a glorious day: bright sunshine and clear waters give you confidence to launch your kayak and paddle around a sheltered bay. Conditions are calm and you glide along smoothly, drifting on balmy blue waves.

Suddenly, you notice the water is becoming choppy and an offshore wind picks up; in what seems like minutes, you find yourself at the mercy of a gale. You and your kayak are being blown out to sea and, as the swell gets higher and rougher, you find you don't have the strength to battle the waves and paddle back to the protection of the bay. Then a big wave capsizes you and you're plunged into cold water. Should you...

A

Try to get back in your kayak or at least partially onto it. Then signal for help using any means at your disposal: VHF radio or mobile phone, wave, use a whistle, shout, let off flares – or a combination of these methods.

B

Abandon your kayak and possessions, and use herculean effort to swim back to shore. Swim hard to keep warm and once back on dry land phone the coastguard to inform them a kayak has been abandoned at sea.

C

Stay with your kayak and wait until the wind has subsided: chances are the weather will clear and you'll be able to get back into the bay without bothering emergency services. Keep your communication device at the bottom of a waterproof bag onboard the kayak so it remains dry for when you need it.

The RNLI suggests kayakers follow these guidelines:

1. Always carry a means of calling for help and keep it on your person.

2. Wear a buoyancy aid.

3. Check the weather and tides – try UKHO Easytide. Be aware of wind strength, especially offshore winds (when the wind is blowing out to sea).

4. If venturing away from the beach, seek knowledge from an expert such as the harbourmaster or lifeguards.

5. Tell someone responsible where you're going and when you'll be back.

6. Wear appropriate clothing for the conditions and your trip, such as a suitable wetsuit/drysuit and layers.

7. Get training to develop your skills – contact your local canoe or kayaking club and look for coaching sessions/paddle awards run by British Canoeing. Learn and practise self-rescue techniques to get back on board your kayak, in case you capsize.

8. Paddle in a group where possible.

9. Check out more detailed RNLI kayak safety advice online at www.rnli.org

10. Download the RYA SafeTrx app and use it to log, track and send alerts about your trip.

Answer

(The answer is **A**)

Try to get back into your kayak – it's important to learn and practise techniques to do this in calm shallow water so when an emergency situation arises you know what to do.

In extreme conditions, if you can only get your body partially out of the water and onto your kayak, it will significantly increase your survival time.

Call for help using whatever means you have at your disposal.

Make sure you have a communication device (such as a mobile phone, a waterproof handheld DSC VHF or a personal locator beacon) on your person. (Remember: if you can't reach it in an emergency, it's no use). When using a mobile phone call 999 or 112 and ask for the coastguard.

Do not attempt to swim to shore and always stay with your kayak – you will make a larger target for the search and rescue groups to find.

Hypothermia

Would you know what to do if a friend developed hypothermia on your camping trip? Army Cadet Ambassador and polar explorer **Craig Mathieson** reveals the dos and the don'ts.

The scenario

You and a friend decide to take a hike across nearby hills and camp out for the night. It's early summer and the weather is good, but during the day you get caught in an unexpected heavy rain shower. As a result you, your friend and your gear are all damp when you set up camp.

You change into dry clothing before getting into your sleeping bag, but your friend decides to retain the heat they've got and layer up more clothes on top of their damp but warm ones.

The temperature drops in the middle of the night and your friend wakes you to complain they're freezing cold and can't warm up. They're shivering, breathing quickly and, when you turn on the torch, you can see they look very pale. Should you ...

A
Tell them to put another layer on top and try and go back to sleep.

B
Get them to change out of their damp clothes and into dry ones. Give them a hot drink and sweets.

C
Take charge and pack up camp with the aim of heading back down the mountain and getting home and into the warm.

Hypothermia 101

❯ Craig says: '*Hypothermia occurs when your body cools down faster than it can stay warm. This can be caused by weather, poor clothing and equipment, lack of food and dehydration.*'

Don't be fooled into thinking that you need to be on a polar expedition to experience hypothermia. Craig reveals that, despite having spent time at the poles in temperatures of -25°c, the coldest he's ever been is in the Cairngorms in Scotland, thanks to the deadly combination of low temperature and high wind-speed.

'*The key to avoiding hypothermia in the first place is preparation,*' says Craig. '*Make sure you have at least one spare set of clothes – including gloves and hat – and lots of food and liquids (I always pack what I know I'll eat, plus double that). Tell people where you're going and exactly where you are going to camp.*

'*Schedule a call home for a certain time so, if you don't ring, your family will know you could be in trouble. Plan for a survival situation wherever you go.*'

Answer

(The answer is **B**)

'*First,*' says Craig, '*check them to see how serious it looks. Shaking is a good sign that their body is working hard to warm them up. Check their skin – is it cold? Do they have blue lips or fingers? Are they confused, slurring, talking nonsense or have a lack of coordination? I've seen a guy shivering violently but telling me he's fine and taking layers off; behaviour can be irrational.*

'*All these are signs of hypothermia and, if you're cadet age, call 999 and ask for an ambulance and they'll put you through to Mountain Rescue. They'll stay on the line and monitor the situation as if they're with you – and rescue you, if needed.*

'*If the person is just shaking, tired, maybe breathing more rapidly and can't get warm but are not confused or uncoordinated, stay calm and reassure them that they'll be fine. I've seen mild hypothermia turn around in five minutes. Speed is of the essence – don't wait for them to go into moderate hypothermia.*

'*It's most important that they get any wet kit off – give them your spare dry kit if you need to, including a dry hat and gloves. While they're doing that, you have time to get the stove on to make them a hot drink. Try to avoid caffeine, but if you already have hot tea in a flask give them that. Hot water is fine, although hot chocolate is better, and give them all the sugary treats you've got with you. Keep talking to them and touch the back of their neck and hands regularly so you can tell if they're warming up.*'

If that doesn't work, call 999.

Any definite no-nos? Craig says: '*Putting every item of their clothing on them and putting them back in their sleeping bag won't work; there needs to be room for air to circulate or they won't warm up.*

'*Also, don't rub their skin hard to try and warm them – it could spark a cardiac arrest.*'

Animal attack

If you needed to outwit a wild foe, would you know what to do? Play dead, fight back ... or leg it?

The scenario

» Shark

You're surfing in the ocean and catching some amazing waves. It's so much fun that you haven't even noticed you've got company. You feel a tug on your leg and look down to discover, to your horror, a shark has its mouth around it. Should you ...

A Play dead

B Defend yourself using as much aggressive force as you can muster

Answer: Defend yourself with whatever weapon you can (avoid using your bare hands or feet if possible). Concentrate your blows on vulnerable spots: the mantra is 'eyes, gills, snout'.

Humans are not natural prey for sharks and once they realise you're not a seal they're likely to spit you out.

» Angry elephant

You're on a jungle trek when, all of a sudden, an aggressive-looking elephant comes running out of the trees in your direction. Should you ...

A Turn your back on the elephant and run

B Climb a tree and hold on tight

Answer: Signs that the animal is in an aggressive mood include pinned-back ears, a lowered head and a curled-in trunk. If the elephant's ears are relaxed it could be a mock charge and you have the option of standing your ground, although their size would influence that decision.

Death is much more likely if you turn your back on a charging elephant and run. One ploy that can work is to climb a tree – just make sure it's too big to be pushed over. And if Jumbo does attack you, play dead until he gets tired of tossing your body around.

» Killer bees

You're out walking with a friend when you suddenly find yourself in the midst of a full-scale attack by a swarm of bees. Should you ...

A Run to the nearest building or car to escape

B Dive into the nearest river, lake or stream

Answer: If you're in the Americas you're in Africanised bee ("killer bee" – pictured) territory and these are much more aggressive than European bees.

They aim for your nose and mouth first, so pull your top over your lower face and leg it. Run as fast and as far as you can and make sure you don't give up too soon – they've been known to chase victims beyond 400 metres. If possible, hide in a building or a car.

Despite what cartoons would have us believe, diving into water is a bad idea – the bees will wait until you come up for air.

If a bee bumps into you it's not an accident; it's a guard bee sent out by a colony to warn predators away. Run before you're attacked by the entire hive.

» Monkey

You're on holiday in India and stop for lunch outside a temple. There are rhesus macaques everywhere and they're rather cute – until one lunges forward, bares its teeth at you and tries to grab your sandwich. Should you ...

A Give it your lunch and pull a funny face

B Scream, wave your arms and try to run away

Answer: Sacrifice your sarnie; they're more interested in eating that than you. Failing that, use the 'open-mouth threat': make an 'O' with your lips, lean forward, raise your eyebrows and then back away slowly.

If that doesn't work, call upon the assistance of the nearest large male (monkeys are more afraid of men than women).

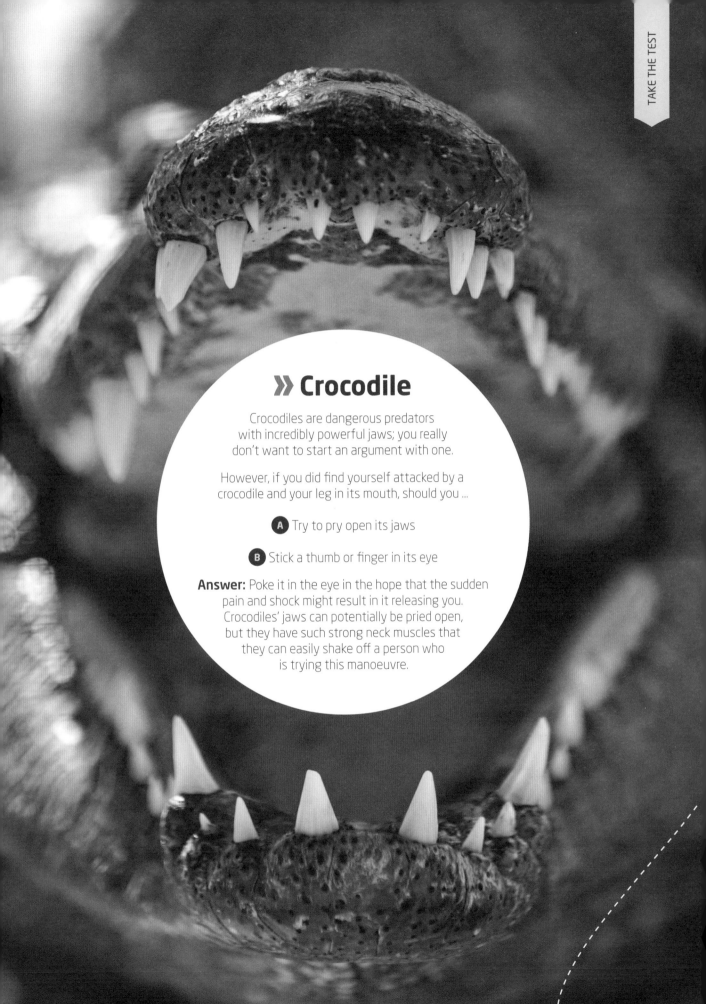

» Crocodile

Crocodiles are dangerous predators with incredibly powerful jaws; you really don't want to start an argument with one.

However, if you did find yourself attacked by a crocodile and your leg in its mouth, should you ...

A Try to pry open its jaws

B Stick a thumb or finger in its eye

Answer: Poke it in the eye in the hope that the sudden pain and shock might result in it releasing you. Crocodiles' jaws can potentially be pried open, but they have such strong neck muscles that they can easily shake off a person who is trying this manoeuvre.

Army Cadets in
December 2019

ACF's Got Talent

After supporting *Britain's Got Talent* winner Colin Thackery on *Songs of Praise*, LNR ACF Corps of Drums were asked to join the 89-year-old Army veteran on stage at the Royal Variety Performance on 10 December. A group of cadet and CFAV drummers performed with Colin in front of the Duke and Duchess of Cambridge – and millions of viewers at home.

Queen's honours

Six CFAVs discovered they had been granted state honours by Her Majesty The Queen when the list of New Year Honours was published in the *London Gazette* on 27 December.

Colonel David Kane and Captain Kim Elizabeth Humberstone were appointed as Officers of the Order of the British Empire (OBE), Lt Colonel Joanne Eccles was awarded Most Excellent Order of the British Empire (MBE) and Captain Bryan Catchpole, Sergeant Major John McMaster and Staff Sergeant Mark Sanders were awarded the British Empire Medal (BEM).

'It is a great privilege and honour to be recognised'

'It was all a little surreal. However, it is a great privilege and honour to be recognised within the New Year Honours,' said Lt Colonel J Eccles MBE.

'This would not have been possible without the amazing team I have around me in Lancashire ACF. They help me push the boundaries to provide our cadets with an amazing experience.'

Conductors' coin

In December, RSM Lily Andrews of Whitefield Detachment became the first cadet to ever receive The Conductors' Coin.

The coin is awarded to individuals who have shown outstanding dedication and have put others before themselves. It's only been awarded to 30 other individuals in the corps. Congratulations Lily.

Walking Home For Christmas

Cadets taking part in the Walking Home for Christmas challenge received an extra surprise for their efforts this year when explorer and Army Major Levison Wood signed every certificate.

The annual campaign, which asks cadets to embark on a challenging walk back to their base, raises money for Walking With The Wounded which supports veterans.

CHALLENGE

Are your survival and map-reading skills good enough to help you navigate – or even stay alive – if you were lost in the wilderness?

On the MAP

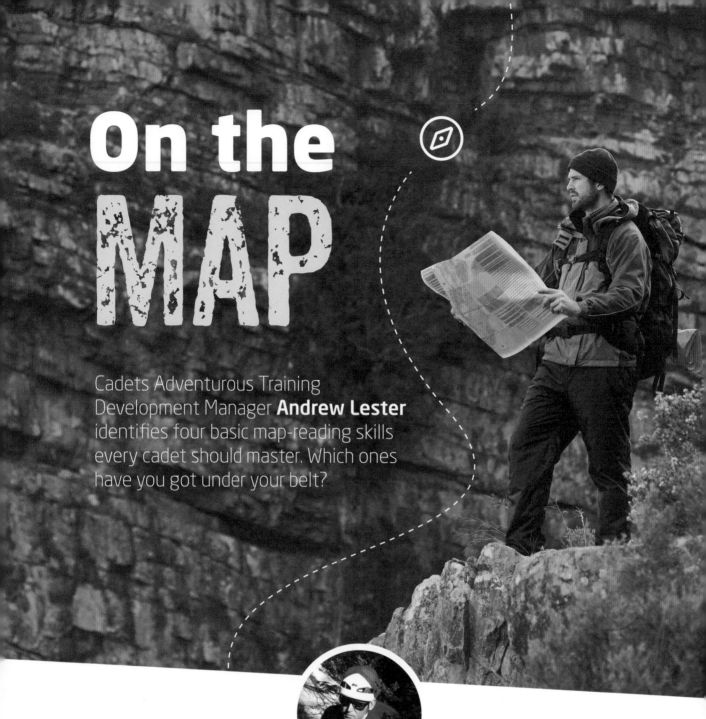

Cadets Adventurous Training Development Manager **Andrew Lester** identifies four basic map-reading skills every cadet should master. Which ones have you got under your belt?

We use navigation skills every day, from following Google Maps when visiting a new city to using satnav while driving. However, despite all the techy developments in mapping, understanding how to navigate a paper Ordnance Survey (OS) map remains a hugely important skill.

Cadets Adventurous Training Development Manager Andrew Lester is a big fan of OS paper maps and says: *'I regularly hear from Mountain Rescue guys about the big problems that occur when people climb mountains using only electronic maps.*

'They're great in their place – especially for planning (you can do your calculations so simply) and as a back up – but it can be easy to misinterpret the scale and run into trouble. And then there are the risks of running out of battery or dropping, breaking or losing the phone on the mountainside.

'Navigation and map-reading are life skills that are extremely useful to have.'

If you think your map-reading skills could do with a brush up, check out the four core navigation skills Andrew thinks every cadet should master.

To Inspire To Achieve

1. Get to grips with grids

Knowing how to pinpoint your exact location using the blue grid lines on an OS map is a key navigational skill and crucial to know if you ever need to call for help in an emergency.

The vertical blue lines are called 'eastings' (they increase in value as you travel east on the map). The horizontal lines are called 'northings' (they increase in value as you travel north on the map).

Four-figure reference

A handy way to identify any square on a map is to use a four-figure reference. Grid references are easy when you remember you always have to go along the corridor before you go up the stairs.

To find the number of a square, first use the eastings (go along the corridor) until you come to the bottom left-hand corner of the square you want. Write down this two-figure number.

Then use the northings (go up the stairs) until you find the bottom left-hand corner of the square. Put this two-figure number after the first one and you have a four-figure grid reference, for example: 6233.

Pinpoint precision

If you want to pinpoint a more precise location on a map, you need to use a six-figure grid reference. First, find the four-figure grid reference for the square you originally identified, then write it down with a space after each set of numbers, like this: 62_ 33_

Now imagine this square is divided up into 100 tiny squares with 10 squares along each side. Still remembering to go along the corridor and up the stairs, work out the extra numbers you need and put them into your four-figure grid reference like this: 625 333.

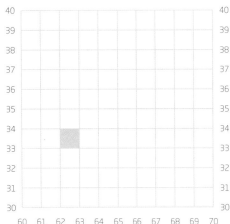

Northings ('up the stairs')

Eastings ('along the corridor')

'Go along the corridor before you go up the stairs'

2. In the distance

It's important to be able to use the scale at the bottom of your map to measure the distance between where you are and where you want to be. You can do this by measuring a distance on the map, comparing it to the scale, and instantly getting a real-world distance.

For straight-line distances on a map, use a ruler to get a measurement between points and then compare it to the map scale.

In real life, your journey might not be a straight line so it's always handy to have a trusty bit of string with you. Lay the string out along the map route, measure, and compare to the scale.

3. Clue up on contours

Being able to visualise the shape of a landscape by looking at the contour lines of a map is a superb navigation tool to master and one that can be easily developed with practice. It's especially essential if you're planning an expedition over mountainous terrain.

'The closer together the contour lines, the steeper the slope of the mountain'

On an OS map, the contour lines (the orange and brown lines) show the height and shape of the landscape. The number on each contour line tells you how high above sea level it is.

Contour lines are the same height all the way along their length, while the height difference between each line is normally 10 metres (your map will tell you the contour interval used). The closer together the contour lines, the steeper the slope of the hill or mountain.

The illustration shows how a landscape is converted into contour lines on a map. It can be helpful to think of contour lines as high tide lines left by the sea: as the water level drops it leaves a line every 10 metres on the landscape. The marks left behind are your contour lines.

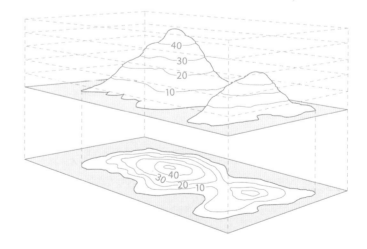

This diagram from *OS Map Reading* illustrates how a landscape is converted into contour lines

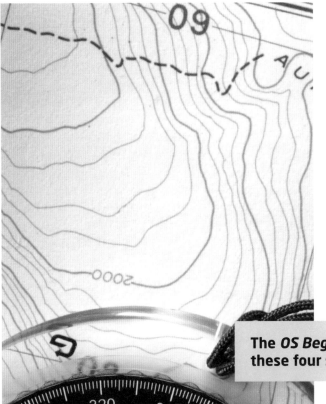

4. Get your bearings

Get to know your compass and it will become an indispensable tool when out hiking, cycling or on expeditions. A compass allows you to navigate accurately when there are few obvious landscape features.

The *OS Beginner's Guide To The Compass* provides these four steps to using a compass for navigation:

» From your starting point on the map, place the index line on an imaginary line between where you are now and where you want to be, with the direction of travel arrow on the base plate pointing the way. Start by drawing a line from A to B.

» Holding the baseplate in place, rotate the compass housing so the orienting arrow lines up with grid north on the map. The orienting lines should be parallel with the vertical blue grid lines (eastings).

» Your compass does not point to grid north. Magnetic north throughout Great Britain can range from 0° to 5°. The amount of variation changes every year, so check your OS map to work out the current value. Add magnetic variation to your bearing by rotating the compass housing.

» Take your compass off the map. Hold your compass flat at waist height and turn yourself until the red needle meets up with the letter N and is positioned over the orienting arrow. You're ready to go and the red direction of travel arrow will point the way.

Thanks to the team at Ordnance Survey for their help with this feature.

Big Phil's
SURVIVAL SKILLS

How would you cope if you found yourself lost in a pitch-black forest without a compass or map? Would you be able to get to grips with hunger, dehydration and exhaustion? Army Cadet Champion **Phil Campion** reveals what it takes to be a survivor.

Nobody is better placed to talk about essential bushcraft than ex-SAS survival expert Big Phil. Drawing on his elite combat experience and a career that has taken him into some of the world's most challenging environments, Phil cites the five most essential skills every cadet should conquer:

'You absolutely need to know how to make a fire, build a shelter, signal for help, find food and clean water, and carry out first aid,' he says. *'Those are the basics of keeping yourself alive and getting help.'*

» Get a grip

He believes the best way to get a grip on them is by getting out on field exercises and practising.

'You can read about them and talk about them but they're the kind of skills you really have to go out into the bush to try out.'

'It's not until you venture out in the real world that you'll see those skills coming alive.'

Phil believes the survivalist mindset you'll learn out in the field will remain with you throughout life and is there to be drawn upon in all kinds of challenging situations.

'When you learn the basics of survival you understand what it is that keeps you alive, happy and well,' he says.

'In the future, when you face a difficult situation, you'll have something to fall back on by asking key questions such as, Why isn't this right?

'If you don't have a foundation in any form of survival, you haven't got a starting point from which to do something about your situation.'

He cites an incident in Norway when the helicopter he was travelling in was forced to make a crash landing.

'The weather was horrendous and two of us had to go and get help while two stayed with the helicopter. It was extremely tough but we made it because we had the right foundations.'

» Preparation

Even on modest expeditions, Phil follows the motto: *'to fail to prepare is to prepare to fail'* which means he always carries water, food, a survival sheet, warm kit, a lighter (or some form of fire starter) and a first-aid kit.

As a young recruit he learnt the hard way what it was like to go out on exercise without being prepared for all eventualities.

'I remember thinking, I'm not going to need this waterproof as it's not going to rain this weekend. It did and I remained wet for the whole time. I put myself in a situation where, had it been a longer exercise, I would have been in a lot of trouble. Not to mention the telling off I got from the corporal.'

'When you learn the basics of survival you understand what it is that keeps you alive, happy and well'

» Kit

The lesson is to have everything you are supposed to and don't cut corners.

'It might weigh a bit more and it might be a little cumbersome, but having the right kit at the right time and in the right place is invaluable,' says Phil.

No-one, of course, relishes being in a situation where they suddenly need to pit themselves against the elements and signal for help, but learning essential survival skills can be an exhilarating challenge.

'Whatever training you do, enjoy it and have fun,' says Phil. *'It's a great subject and one that could take you in many different directions. Learn it properly and it'll stay with you for the rest of your life – and could actually save it.'*

BIG PHIL'S BIG 5

1. Food and water

'*Without food and water there are obvious repercussions*,' says Phil.

Your body won't survive much longer than three days without liquids, so knowing how to collect, filter and sterilise water is essential.

In contrast, your body can survive for up to three weeks without food. However, eating provides the energy required to carry out all the other survival skills. Luckily, nature supplies food to fuel up on (see right).

2. Signalling

'*To survive, you're going to have to get help from somebody,*' says Phil.

From the outset of a survival situation, you need to keep rescue scenarios front of mind. Attracting attention to yourself is key and there are a variety of ways to do this: fire and smoke, flashlights, brightly coloured clothing, reflective mirrors and whistles. Three of anything is the traditional way to signal for help: three blows of a whistle, three flashes of a light or three sticks in the shape of a triangle.

Devising an effective way to signal for help in an emergency could save your life.

Five common edible plants

Navelwort or pennywort (pictured) is a succulent with a high water content, which tends to grow in shady spots and on dry stone walls. Pick the new growth as these shoots will taste the sweetest and won't have been damaged by insects.

Goosegrass is the plant that produces the sticky buds which cling to your clothes after a walk in the woods. Its tender shoots are best cooked but can be eaten raw.

Brambles/blackberries are great as not only can you eat the berries, you can also eat the shoots of these spiky plants. Peel back the thorns and leaves to find a tasty green tip.

Dandelion is versatile: roast the roots to make "coffee", nibble the stems, make tea from the flowers and snack on the leaves. Choose new growth as the older leaves taste bitter.

Stinging nettles can be boiled over fire to make a tea (the warmth of the fire will neutralise the sting).

3. First aid

'*You need a basic level of first aid to be in a position to help others and yourself,*' says Phil.

Always take a first-aid kit on any expedition and make sure you know how to effectively use it for cuts, bruises and injuries. Carry a survival sheet in your kit and know how to treat conditions caused by the elements, such as frostbite, hypothermia, heat exhaustion and sunburn.

First aid is not just crucial in a survival situation of course – accidents can happen anywhere.

4. Shelter

'*You'll need to find shelter from the rain and sun,*' says Phil.

The first type of shelter to think about is clothing: choose wisely according to the environment you're likely to find yourself in and be sure to dress in layers to maximise your ability to adapt to changing conditions.

Being exposed to the elements for too long – just a few hours in extremely harsh weather conditions – will rapidly lead to a downward spiral in your ability to perform tasks.

Knowing how and where to pitch a tent, build an emergency shelter or erect a basha is essential. When out in the field, practise techniques to build shelters so you'd feel equipped and confident in an emergency.

5. Fire

'*You need fire for warmth and cooking,*' says Phil.

It provides heat, light and comfort in a survival situation. It will cook your food, purify water, discourage wild animals, dry out wet clothing and boost morale.

It's important to know how to spot and gather the three main things to build and maintain a fire – tinder, kindling and fuelwood – and to practise different methods to light it.

Army Cadets in
January 2020

First ever National ACF Conference takes place

The first National ACF conference was a seminal moment for the organisation and provided a great opportunity to bring together 300 senior leaders to discuss how to take Army Cadets into the 21st century.

© Kate Knight

» The conference at Royal Military Academy Sandhurst was also the perfect occasion to announce two new adventuresome ambassadors: Gulf War veteran Craig Mathieson and Afghanistan veteran Major (Retd) Sally Orange (read about both ambassadors on pages 19-20).

The pair were welcomed to the ACF family in front of more than 300 people.

'I'm so excited to have been given this opportunity,' said Craig after the event. *'I look forward to developing my role and working with cadets and CFAVs over the coming months.'*

Sally Orange was also honoured and privileged to have been asked to be the first female National Ambassador for the ACF.

'To work with such an incredible youth organisation and help influence young people in such a positive manner is something I strongly believe in,' she said.

Another important highlight of the day was the talk by Professor Simon Denny of the University of Northampton who shared the

© Kate Knight

findings of his study into the benefits of the cadet experience. He revealed that being a member of the Cadet Forces significantly improves outcomes in education and contributes to lifelong learning, success and development. Read more about his conclusions on page 89.

Officer Cdt Caddick also gave an inspiring speech about Army Cadet experiences and his more recent time at Sandhurst. Attendees were introduced to the new Cadet portal.

General Eastman welcomed as new Commander Cadets

We were delighted to welcome Major General David Eastman as our new Commander Cadets this month. Find out more about him on page 74.

INSPIRING PEOPLE

Learn life lessons from Aldo Kane (pictured), discover what Commander Cadets Major General David Eastman MBE has to say about leadership, meet Major Heidi MacLeod, and learn how former Army cadet Jas Shergill grabbed opportunities with both hands.

» Major General David Eastman MBE, Commander Cadets

Were you a cadet?

I was a staff sergeant in the CCF at Edinburgh School (an Army school) in Germany where we lived. My dad, a band sergeant major in the Cavalry, was stationed there. Then I went to Welbeck College (the defence 6th form college for technical officers) where I was the bandmaster in the CCF.

'Being a cadet was the launchpad for my entire career'

Music has been a big part of my life ever since: I've played the cornet, bass guitar, piano, saxophone – whatever the local band didn't have.

What were you like as a teenager?

I got involved in everything: I was out every evening at Cadets, Scouts or the choir, or playing football for a local German team – my parents never saw me.

If you met your teenage self now, what would you tell him?

Not to be constrained by other people's ideas or expectations.

What did you get out of being in the Army Cadets?

It was the first time I had any kind of responsibility or experience of working with other people. It taught me teamwork, discipline, humility and how to deal with others. It was a chance to learn by making mistakes.

One of the most important things I learnt was that, as the leader, you are not the arbiter of ideas: the aim is to get the best out of the people who work for you and you do that by treating them with respect. It's not about that traditional sergeant major style of shouting at people.

The reason I am where I am now is because of the Cadets and, notably, my detachment commander at Edinburgh School CCF. He gave me the confidence to apply to become an officer (I was the first in my family).

I didn't have a great deal of confidence and, coming from the background I did, becoming an officer wasn't something that was expected. He advised me to take one step at a time and told me I had as good a chance of succeeding as anyone; I applied for Welbeck as a result.

Being a cadet was the launchpad for my entire career.

On exercise at Edinburgh School, Germany, 1985

Do you think leadership is natural or can it be learnt?

Some people naturally possess the skills, but I think anyone can learn how to become a leader.

There are a few key things to learn: the first is about humility and treating others with respect, the second is being able to communicate with people, and the third is understanding the "why". I read an interesting book by Simon Sinek called *Start With Why* and I always try and lead with that.

How did your Army career begin?

I got into Welbeck College, ended up going to Sandhurst for officer training and joined the REME [Royal Electrical and Mechanical Engineers].

I've had the most amazing career: I've been a paratrooper commando, a helicopter engineer, commanded a tank-repair battalion, and I've been deployed to Afghanistan, Iraq, Bosnia, Kosovo and Northern Ireland.

In the last seven years I've been all over the world for various reasons. I was head of International Policy and Plans for Sub-Saharan Africa, Latin America and the Caribbean, and I've just spent a year in Australia doing their strategic studies course.

My first placement was in Hong Kong where I spent a year chasing illegal immigrants on BMX bikes coming across the border from China. Then I was sent to Nepal where I had to fix hospital equipment in 22 mission hospitals across the country.

'Sitting on a boulder in the middle of the jungle, surrounded by hippos, responding to emails ... '

I've been really lucky in the jobs I've had – one of them was commanding a brigade responsible for counter-poaching in southern Africa, so I was in Malawi setting up counter-poaching training for the rangers. I remember sitting on a boulder in the middle of the jungle, surrounded by hippos, responding to emails on my laptop ...

Which has been the most challenging period of your career?

When I was the Deputy Chief of Staff of 16 Air Assault Brigade when we first went into Helmand in Afghanistan. I was supposed to go for six weeks to get the brigade in and then return home – I came back seven months later.

The tour didn't go the way we expected. The lesson for me there was the truism that 'plans never survive contact' and that was absolutely the case; nothing turned out the way we'd planned, so we had to react to what was facing us on the ground.

That was a very hard tour for me, which goes back to leadership. You have to get the best out of the people around you, understand why you are there and what you are trying to achieve, then get ideas from everyone on how to deliver. It was an object lesson in doing that.

What's your mindset when things go wrong?

The Army is very good at training you to plan in the absence of knowledge – or 'the fog of war' as we call it – and to quickly come to some kind of conclusion.

I've just spent six months commanding the Defence Covid Force. We had a thousand planners out across the country supporting local government departments. The skill they brought to the table wasn't the expertise of the NHS or the Department of Health and Social Care, but the ability to plan quickly without full knowledge of what was happening.

Army cadet at Edinburgh School CCF (far right), 1985

On that first tour in Helmand Province, Afghanistan

What's your day job right now?

My boss, General Ty [Lieutenant General Tyrone Urch CBE, Commander Home Command], has taken over the command of the Defence Covid Force so I'm his deputy for that and then my real day job is General Officer Commanding Regional Command. My job is to enable the Army to live, train and operate. I run the stations and garrisons; I run our support to British troops in Nepal, Brunei and Germany; and I provide all the facilities management across our organisation.

I also do all our defence engagement for the UK, and our resilience operations – so if there's a fire or a flood, it's our organisation that responds to that. And, of course, I'm also Commander Cadets.

By what ethos do you try to live?

The Army values and standards have been instilled in me for my entire career, so that's it. However, I also believe that looking after your people is key, wherever you are and whatever you're doing. I've never understood the aggressive leadership thing because people naturally recoil – you don't get the best out of anybody.

> *'At home you try and switch off the military thing and become a civilian'*

Does your job influence the way you live your family life?

I have four teenagers so I suspect they'd say 'yes'. At home you try and switch off the military thing and become a civilian. You don't want to treat your children as if you're at work but, if you stick to that ethos of treating people with respect, you can't go wrong.

My eldest is at Welbeck and the other three, because we move every two years, are at boarding school. So, when we do see them, the last thing you want is to be at loggerheads.

What piece of adventurous training would you like to undertake if time and money were no object?

I love parachuting: I did the parachuting course for the Army and I did sport parachuting when I was in Hong Kong and Cyprus, so I reckon that would be it if I were in the UK. Otherwise ... well, I'm a skier and chair of REME Ice Sports and I have to undertake luge and bobsleigh, so that's what I'll end up doing next – whether I like it or not!

In post as Commander Cadets

Favourite way to spend a weekend?

Out with the kids and the dog, walking the hills.

2020 has been an extremely unusual year ...

I do feel for our cadets who have been frustrated, but we've seen some great innovations in terms of adult volunteers delivering virtual sessions and the fabulous things that cadets have been doing. I just sent a Commander's Coin to a cadet who spent the whole of lockdown living in an Anderson shelter to raise money. The resilience shown by the cadets has been amazing.

One of the things we're looking to achieve with the Cadets organisation is the idea of creating a better citizen who contributes to society. Cadets is a mechanism to do that, while having fun and a bit of action at the same time.

The pandemic has also been a real opportunity for people to get involved in lateral thinking and come up with innovative ideas about how to provide support and keep themselves involved. It enabled me to do an online talk and Q&A with the Scottish Cadets. It was a connection I probably wouldn't have made before the pandemic, so it's opened up new ways of connecting.

Finally, what piece of kit couldn't you do without?

My Asics trainers; I love my physical exercise.

» Major Heidi MacLeod

Major Heidi was the first woman to command a troop of 70 Gurkhas in the Queen's Own Gurkha Logistic Regiment (QOGLR). She tells us about her historic first and reveals the challenges and opportunities that have come with her career.

'I'm grateful for the map-reading skills I learned in the CCF'

Major Heidi retracing the steps of the Heroes of Telemark across the Norwegian Hardangervidda

What did it feel like to be the first woman to command a troop of Gurkhas in the QOGLR?

I felt immensely proud and very privileged, and hoped other females would follow in my footsteps.

What attracted you to the Gurkhas?

I wanted the challenge of learning a new culture and language, as well as the chance to lead a group of highly motivated and fit men.

Tell us about the Gurkhas' iconic weapon

Kukris are curved knives with a wide blade that are functional multi-purpose tools. They are carried on the webbing of serving Gurkha soldiers and officers – and also feature on every Gurkha cap badge. The knives have a ceremonial role too and are used in kukri dances.

What qualities does a troop leader need?

You need to be bright and confident in order to inspire others to be motivated to work for you. You must know your team, show compassion, be respectful and non-judgemental, and know their strengths and weaknesses in order to get the best out of them. Above all, you need to lead by example and show high standards of self-discipline, honesty and integrity.

What have been your biggest career challenges?

Sleep deprivation was always a challenge in training – though it's amazing what little sleep you can survive and function on.

'Doors have opened for women in all areas of the Army'

Earning the respect of my first troop and taking them safely on operational tours to Kosovo and Iraq (during the initial invasion in 2003) were two of my biggest professional challenges.

I've also faced tough physical challenges as part of the Army Mount Everest West Ridge Expedition in 2006, the first Army Ladies Fastnet Sailing Team in 2013 and, more recently, while retracing the steps of the Heroes of Telemark across the Norwegian Hardangervidda.

Did you learn Nepalese when you joined the Gurkhas?

I learned conversational Nepalese and also had the opportunity to trek to remote parts of Nepal to visit Gurkha veterans as part of my language training. I'm not a natural linguist and found the listening skills the most difficult. I'm certainly not fluent.

What did you learn as a cadet which has been useful in your career?

I remember having to be smartly dressed in our uniform for inspections and that required self-pride and self-discipline. I'm still self-disciplined and rise at 5.30am to do my fitness training before work.

I am also very grateful for the map-reading skills I learned in the CCF which helped me become a Mountain Leader.

What did you find difficult as a cadet?

I was daunted about going away on CCF summer camps and completing the assault course but, once I stopped worrying and got stuck in, it was extremely enjoyable and rewarding.

It's very easy to talk yourself out of doing something you're not confident about, for fear of failure or looking silly, but life is too short not to make the most of every opportunity presented to you – it shapes and develops you as a person. I still grasp every opportunity made available to me at work.

What are the opportunities like for women in the armed forces?

Very recently doors have opened for women to serve in all areas of the Army, including combat roles previously limited to men. The first female infantry officer was commissioned in August 2019.

Currently there are no females serving in the elite 22 Special Air Service but women do work in Special Forces roles in the Special Forces Reconnaissance Regiment.

SMASHING
BOUNDARIES
» Aldo Kane

The TV adventurer and former Royal Marines commando sniper shares eight powerful techniques which have enabled him to overcome fears and smash boundaries.

It's fair to say Aldo Kane knows a thing or two about facing fear: he's been held at gunpoint, charged by a black rhino, spent ten days locked in an abandoned nuclear bunker and abseiled into an active volcano. And, as a location expert for the TV and film industry, his job has seen him come face-to-face with danger in some of the most far-flung places on the planet.

With each action-packed adventure comes the opportunity to learn physically demanding new skills: he's spent days on big walls with top climbers, hunted killer viruses in the darkest corners of the Congo, explored remote caverns with expert cavers, and skydived with the world's elite.

To build the physical and mental resilience necessary to overcome his fears and stretch his comfort zone, Aldo follows a strict goal-setting regime, ensuring that he can turn up ready for action, anywhere in the world, with the right mindset and set of skills.

'You will become what you think about yourself'

Want to be more Aldo? Read his blueprint for smashing boundaries and overcoming fears.

1. Know what you want to achieve

Aldo advises everyone to take time out to decide what they want to achieve in life and create a vision that really inspires them.

'Some people give more consideration to where they want to go on their summer holidays than what they want to do with the rest of their lives,' he chuckles.

At the age of 16, Aldo dedicated all his spare time outside of school to getting fit and strong so he could pursue his dream of joining the Royal Marines. A tough daily training regime prepared him to take on what he describes as 'the hardest infantry training in the world'.

Having clear goals later in life also enabled him to smash two world records by rowing across the Atlantic from mainland Europe to South America.

2. Break goals down

Aldo recommends spending time thinking about the target you want to achieve, then breaking it down into a series of small steps.

'If a dream is so far out it seems completely unattainable, it's easy to let it slip by the wayside,' he says. 'The way I have operated over the years is to have a massive goal and then break it down into steps I can achieve in both the short and long term.'

3. Know your "why"

He stresses the importance of not only knowing *what* you want to achieve but also the reasons *why* you want to achieve it.

'*It's not difficult to eat an apple a day but it's also difficult to eat an apple a day*' is his paradoxical maxim.

'*If it's wet, cold and raining outside and the "why" isn't big enough, you're not going to be driven and motivated to get up and do those smaller bite-size chunks.*

'*It's all about that drive to get up every single day and work towards your goal – and that will only happen if you are motivated because the "why" is big enough.'*

4. Mitigate the risk of failure

Aldo suggests writing down all the obstacles and scary situations you could possibly encounter along the way to reaching your goal and thinking about the best ways to overcome them.

'*You can never fully know or understand what might happen in the future but, if you are well trained and well prepared, you can deal with all the eventualities that might get thrown at you.*

'*On expeditions we do many things to mitigate the risk of failure. If we are white-water kayaking, we learn how to white-water kayak, how to rescue from boats and how to live on the side of a river safely. It all comes down to planning and the military adage: "If you fail to plan, you plan to fail".'*

5. Understand your fear

Aldo believes fear is a natural and vital response to the threat of danger: an important emotion which has the potential to save you from death. However, when pursuing your goal you shouldn't let fear paralyse you and rob you of your dream.

It's crucial to assess whether your fear is justified (ie the threat is real) or whether you're experiencing an irrational fear.

'*Opinion is quite a good way of compounding fear and making the situation much worse than it actually is,*' he says. '*In scary times I always try to mentally take myself away from the situation and find a place in my head where I can start dealing with the facts.*

'*A good phrase is "control the controllables". When something scary happens, you may not be able to physically control the situation, people or kit, but you can control your feelings and reactions.*

'*Fear is there for a reason and it's super helpful – but it shouldn't be the controller of your life and decisions.'*

6. Train for resilience

He suggests getting out in the field and using physical and mental training in the outdoors to build resilience, stretching your comfort zone in challenging environments such as mountains and moorland.

'*Whether you are at elite level or just leaving the house for the first time in six weeks, the fundamentals to building resilience are the same: take yourself physically, mentally and emotionally out of your comfort zone in a controlled manner. The more you do that, the more resilient you'll become and then, when you do face a crisis, you'll be able to cope.'*

'Take yourself out of your comfort zone in a controlled manner'

7. Cultivate a positive mindset

It's Aldo's belief that anyone can do anything they put their mind to.

'The first thing I say to young people when I speak to them is "you will literally become what you think about yourself".

'If you are filling your head with negative thoughts, then your life will be a fairly negative place and you'll have trouble achieving your goals. Everyone is where they are because of the way they think.'

8. Embrace your failures

Despite his phenomenal achievements, Aldo doesn't get stressed about getting things wrong, believing experience doesn't come from getting something perfect but from bad judgment and mistakes.

'I fail all the time,' he says. *'I fail on expeditions and I fail as a person and a friend. But I am not my failures, so if I fail at something it doesn't bother me for the rest of my life – or even the rest of the day. It's just something that happened.'*

He cites the example of a heat-seeking missile: despite making errors left and right, it always corrects itself back onto target.

'It's quite a good analogy for life,' he says. *'If you're too scared to do something because you are worried about making mistakes or what someone else might think of you, you'll never get off the starting block.*

'I've always thought the sooner I make a mistake, the sooner I understand what the mistake was about and the sooner I can rectify it and be ahead of the game. Success breeds mistakes and mistakes breed success.'

Stretch to success

» Jas Shergill

Natural talent may give you a head start when it comes to leadership but, as **Jas Shergill** explains, it's seizing opportunities that really leads to success.

D
o you need to be a "born leader" to teach and guide others? Not according to pharmacy student Jas Shergill. The 20-year-old former Army cadet, who is studying at Keele University, worked her way up through the ranks of the CCF – smashing a few female-firsts along the way – by taking on new responsibilities, building experience and learning new skills.

Jas's path to leadership began in Year 12 when she joined the after-school CCF at Queen Mary's Grammar School in Walsall.

'I was the first to sign up after a recruitment drive,' says Jas. *'I've always had a hands-on type of personality, but I also wanted to challenge stereotypes and do things that a girl – even in my generation – would not be expected to do.'*

Her willingness to step up was noticed by her contingent officers who asked her to join the teaching rota. By November she was tutoring others in drill skills she herself had only started to learn in September.

'I am quite a driven person: the idea of taking on responsibility was drilled into me from a very young age and, for that, I thank my parents and grandparents,' she says. *'It was my maternal grandmother who taught me to rise above prejudice, and my paternal grandfather who taught me to do everything wholeheartedly.'*

To Inspire To Achieve

The following summer Jas was given the role of section commander at her first annual camp (at Longmoor in Hampshire). During the two weeks of challenges, she encouraged her team to do their best in everything from reconnaissance patrols and orienteering to fieldcraft stalks, and camouflage and concealment.

'Before the awards ceremony I told my team that, regardless of whether they received recognition or not, I was proud of the amount of effort and energy they had put into every activity.

'The amazing thing was we won! In my state of shock, my section carried me to the front where I was presented with the Section Commander Trophy – I was the first female to have their name engraved on it.'

Jas's success was echoed later that autumn when she was presented with the 210 Battery Trophy, an

'By the end of my time with the CCF I was able to plan and execute a night-time platoon defence'

honour given to the cadet with the best individual military skills.

Her next big opportunity came when she was invited to be platoon commander during a tactics weekend.

'I was very surprised and actually didn't want it, but our contingent commander said: "you'll do it well because you care and teach". It was this continuous support and encouragement from the contingent officers that gave me the motivation to take on more and more responsibility.'

Jas is extremely grateful for the opportunities that came her way

during her time in the CCF. Although she took part in other programmes, such as the Duke of Edinburgh's Award and National Citizen Service, it was the incremental progression of the CCF that helped her develop into the leader she is today. She is now a full-time student but still keeps her hand in as a sergeant instructor.

'The scope for students to take on responsibility and grow independently is something the CCF and ACF do best. Working through the ranks gives students something to aim for, but along the way they gain so much more than just reaching the next rank.

'Joining the CCF was a life-changing experience which taught me so much about myself. It gave me confidence and motivated me – skills I call upon every day.'

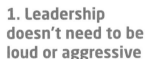

JAS'S LEADERSHIP 101

1. Leadership doesn't need to be loud or aggressive

'Leadership is often seen as a way of enforcing authority and trying to manage everyone within a group. However, my experience has taught me that being a good leader means passing tasks down the chain of command to effectively work towards a goal.'

2. Work as a team

'I always felt I really belonged in the CCF. I remember on one platoon attack I was running

across difficult terrain and fell. What made me smile was seeing the rest of my section, to the left and right of me, also falling to the ground alongside me.'

3. Be resilient

'The CCF teaches you to recover quickly from setbacks. Resilience is something I've used in many day-to-day situations – from an exam not going as expected to facing difficulties.'

4. Be confident

'The CCF provided me with endless opportunities to come

up with ideas and strategies and my officers would often say "go for it". Initially I was nervous to put my strategies into operation, even with a small patrol, but by the end of my time with the CCF I was able to plan and execute a night-time platoon defence.

'The ability to put my thoughts into action is something I continue to draw upon in my work with the Army Cadets' cultural diversity Step Change project which aims to prevent and remove discrimination within the ACF and the CCF.'

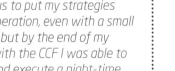
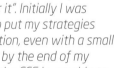

Army Cadets in
February 2020

'Benefits of being a cadet were revealed: improved social mobility, more effective education, improved wellbeing, and enhanced employability'

To Inspire To Achieve

Cadet experience helps young people climb higher

The Combined Cadet Force Headteachers Conference took place on 27 February.

The one-day event was an opportunity for headteachers, CCF leaders and interested parties to spend a day discussing how to maximise the positive impact CCF has on schools, cadets and the community.

Professor Simon Denny of the University of Northampton

© Carl Recine

The Right Honourable Gavin Williamson MP, Secretary of State for Education, was the keynote speaker at the event and said: *'Our armed forces are the best in the world, and what they do in terms of working with our schools is amazing. CCF makes a real difference to children up and down the country and I'm proud that, last year, we hit our target of creating 500 Combined Cadet Forces. These give young people the chance to learn technical skills, leadership skills, a sense of belonging and confidence to achieve the very best for their futures.'*

He revealed the aim to further increase the number of CCF detachments so that 60,000 young people would be part of the organisation.

Also at the conference, Professor Simon Denny of the University of Northampton presented the findings of his study into the impact of the Cadet experience on social mobility.

He found the Cadet experience contributes positively to improvements in wellbeing, confidence, resilience and independence, and that being a cadet improves the behaviour and school attendance of young people – leading to associated attainment benefits for them and society as a whole.

The main benefits were revealed: improved social mobility, more effective education (school, wellbeing and connectedness), improved mental and physical wellbeing and enhanced employability (for both cadets and CFAVs).

On attempting to identify the return on the government's investment in the Cadet movement, the study calculated a saving of £83m per annum to the Treasury. This is as a result of cadets being more likely to access higher or further education (therefore paying more in taxes), and having better physical and mental health (therefore costing the NHS less).

Significant savings are also made as a result of reducing the lifetime amount of money spent on people as a result of exclusion.

WELLBEING

Exercise (especially outdoors), good nutrition
and looking after our mental health are the
foundations of wellbeing. Read on for ideas from
the experts on how to be your best self in 2021.

Mind games

Everyone knows that going for a run, hike or cycle is good for physical health, but how often do you lace up your trainers specifically to improve your mental health? We talked to ex-professional snowboarder and CALM trustee and ambassador **Marcus Chapman**.

Before becoming a trustee and ambassador for mental health charity CALM, Marcus Chapman travelled the world as a sponsored snowboarder. And it was at the beginning of his boarding career he met his best friend Nelson Pratt who went on to coach the Army snowboard team and Olympic bronze medallist Jenny Jones.

In 2006 Nelson took his own life, which came as a huge shock to his family, friends and the British snowboarding community. Following Nelson's death, Marcus and Nelson's brother Chris set up a cycling event called Nelson's Tour de Test Valley in order to mark his memory and raise awareness of male suicide.

How did you get into snowboarding?

'I didn't do amazingly in my A Levels, so after I finished school I decided to do a snowboard season in Tignes, France. My parents said I had to get some sort of qualification so I trained as a snowboard instructor and worked as a night porter in the evenings – and that's how I met Nelson.

'We were flat buddies and became pretty inseparable. We both qualified as instructors that season and ended up staying in Tignes for a few years, becoming sponsored snowboarders. We were given a travel budget, worked with photographers and basically got paid to jump off stuff for a living. We had a brilliant time and, on reflection, that was when I really started to

'As sponsored snowboarders we got paid to jump off stuff for a living'

become aware of my own mental health: how good being in the mountains and doing a sport I loved made me feel.

'Nelson went on to coach the Army snowboard team for a number of years and also Jenny Jones whom he helped win a bronze medal in the 2014 Sochi Olympics – the UK's first ever medal on snow. Following a couple of injuries, I went on to edit *Snowboard UK* which was Britain's biggest snowboarding magazine.'

How did you get involved with CALM?

'I knew that Nelson had had some low points and

struggled with his mental health previously, but his death came as a massive shock.

'His brother Chris and I wanted to do something to honour Nelson and reduce the stigma around suicide and mental health issues. So we launched a cycle sportive and that's how I came across CALM. Nelson's Tour de Test Valley has now been running for eight years and raised over £500,000 for the charity.

Above: Pro snowboarder Nelson Pratt

Left: Marcus on the cover of *Snowboard UK*

Olympic snowboarders Jenny Jones and Aimee Fuller at Tour de Test Valley

Right: Marcus (right) with Chris Pratt at the 2018 sportive

'What impressed us about CALM is that it manages to reach a younger audience and talks directly about mental health and suicide. The charity uses a lot of positive language and ambassadors, and gives people hope. The message is always that there is absolutely no shame in coming forward and by talking together we're stronger.'

Why is talking about mental health important?

'It's so easy to get in your own head and believe what you tell yourself. Your thoughts can become powerful and cruel and there's research to show they can become irrational. It sounds so simple but if you're able to talk to someone about those thoughts, it can help you to realise they aren't true and start to understand them.

'If you choose to speak to someone you know, hearing them say 'I'm struggling too' is really powerful and it can be comforting to know you're not alone. If your mate or someone you respect says 'I had those same thoughts last week' it reinforces that you're not failing or unusual. I've struggled and not wanted to talk to anyone, then as soon as I start talking about it I remember the power of talking and think, *Why didn't I do that sooner?'*

'Everyone struggles with their mental health at some point'

What role does sport play in maintaining good mental health?

'Research shows that exercise can have as big an effect as antidepressants and some other treatments - it's absolutely crucial to our mental health.

'Doing some sort of exercise in the morning – whether that's a run, swim, walk or cycle – has been proven to improve how we sleep. The amount of sleep we get is the absolute bedrock of good mental health; just one night of poor sleep can increase anxiety levels.

'Exercise at the right time (exercising late at night can raise stress hormones) not only aids sleep, it also provides a form of escape.

'"Mindfulness" has become something of a buzzword, but going for a walk or run can be a source of mindfulness because your brain is focusing on what you're doing – you're breathing rhythmically and serotonin is being released.'

What advice would you give to people struggling with their mental health?

'It's important to know that everyone struggles with their mental health at some point. If you're really struggling (ie not sleeping, having panic attacks, feeling very anxious all the time or having suicidal thoughts) you should seek medical help from a doctor.

'For someone who's feeling a bit down or struggling with anxiety from time to time, the first step is to find someone you feel comfortable talking to.

'Professional athletes often use breathing exercises before competing'

'It's often easier talking to someone you don't know because there's no expectation or history between you, so that's where something like CALM's helpline or web chat comes in handy.

'It sounds corny, but doing simple breathing exercises can also really help with sleep and anxiety – the four-second box is a good tool (breath in for four seconds, hold for four seconds, breath out for four seconds and repeat). Professional athletes and sportspeople often use it before competing as it slows down the heart rate and lowers blood pressure.

'More broadly, focusing on having a really good routine is beneficial. It sounds boring but making sure you get enough sleep and making time to do exercise are small changes that can really improve your mental health.'

Getting help

For more information on mental health services or to talk to someone:

CALM
0800 58 58 58
(lines open 5pm-12am)

YoungMinds
YoungMinds Crisis Messenger:
Text YM to 85258
(free 24/7 support across the UK for young people experiencing a mental health crisis)

Parents Helpline: 0808 802 5544
(Monday to Friday 9.30am-4pm)

Homefront phys

Want to stay fit and strong but bored of your current routine? Check out these energising ways to shake up your training and try something new.

›› Social running

Find that boredom sets in and cuts your run short when going solo? If you crave some friendly competition, there's an app that enables runners to virtually join friends on their run in real time, wherever they are in the world.

Racefully is free and, whether you want to race, compare stats or just have some company on your jog, it's a brilliant way to connect with friends or race in teams.

The 'street workout'

You don't need dumbbells or a kettlebell to build muscle; gravity and your own body weight are the only equipment required in **calisthenics**.

You may not have heard of the training movement (or know how to pronounce it) but you will have seen people doing it: human flags (raising the body parallel to the ground while holding a pole) and muscle-ups (raising the whole body above the bar when performing pull-ups) are both examples.

A mix of gymnastics and body-weight training, the 'street workout' is gathering a growing following online.

Like any sport or exercise regime, you need to begin with the basics: start by working on your form and technique in compound movements such as push-ups, squats and planks. You can find lots of easy-to-follow tutorials online.

» Take a virtual ride

Always wanted to ride around the Italian lakes or take on the epic routes of the Alps? Don't let travel restrictions squash your ambition – all you need are a screen and a **Turbo Trainer** and you can complete the world's best cycling routes from your living room.

Turbo Trainers allow you to turn a regular bike into a stationary machine. Basic versions cost around £50, while snazzy models can also control resistance and give stats on your ride. Once set up in front of a screen, choose your virtual route on YouTube and get pedalling.

Try Muay Thai

The national sport of Thailand **Muay Thai** is an ancient martial art which uses the body as a weapon. While today it's practised as a sport instead of for defence, Thai boxing is fast paced and, like boxing, can be dangerous if not done responsibly.

However, the basic movements in Muay Thai can be great for coordination, cardio and mobility. Find a local club to spar with a partner or learn the shadow boxing basics at home via YouTube.

» Stay fit – British Army style

To help keep personnel fit during lockdown, the **Royal Army Physical Training Corps** put together a series of home workout routines.

The collection of weekly workouts are available to browse online. The videos include simple (although tough) repetitions – with no kit required.

Watch them at:
www.army.mod.uk/home-fitness

» Yoga, but not as you know it

If you want to develop flexibility as well as strength, but don't feel yoga is for you, **yogability** may be the answer.

The blend of yoga and mobility was devised by Welsh international rugby union player Alecs Donovan as a way to work on flexibility while also maintaining muscle. The sessions are definitely more sweat than zen and focus on areas such as hip mobility and handstand progression, as well as full body flow.

Join one of Alecs' live online classes at www.yogability.fit

Mental health workout

Regular training keeps our bodies in peak physical condition, but there are also activities we can do to help maintain good mental health, says counsellor and psychotherapist **Kelly Smith**.

〉 1. Stick to a regular sleep cycle

Maintaining a regular sleep cycle is hugely important for good mental health.

'The natural human circadian rhythm is actually 24 hours and 15 minutes, so if we allow ourselves to sleep too much, we eventually tend towards becoming nocturnal,' says Kelly. *'We need as many daylight hours as possible and a minimum of eight hours sleep per 24 to thrive.*

'I'm afraid napping isn't great as it puts our sleep cycle out of kilter,' adds Kelly. *'Going to sleep and getting up at regular times really is the bedrock for both physical and mental health.'*

〉 2. Give yourself premium-grade fuel

It can be easy to comfort eat when you're feeling a bit low, but eating healthily is actually a much better way to boost mood.

'Our bodies work best when well rested and fuelled with the right foods,' says Kelly. *'Eighty per cent of our brain is in our gut, so we really are what we eat. Our sense of wellbeing depends on it.'*

The same applies to what we drink. *'Avoid too many caffeinated and fizzy drinks and stay hydrated by drinking plenty of water,'* says Kelly.

'Eighty per cent of our brain is in our gut, so we really are what we eat. Our sense of wellbeing depends on it'

Merseyside ACF
© Carl Recine

❭ 3. Prioritise connection

'When we're stressed, alongside the release of cortisol (which can lead us to feel anxious and restless) our bodies create a hormone called oxytocin – sometimes known as the "cuddle hormone" – which tells us to connect with others and share our feelings,' says Kelly.

Face-to-face connection is best of all – and one of the benefits of being part of an Army Cadet detachment – but any connection is good.

Thanks to technology, it's never been easier to stay in touch with friends and family, even when social distancing measures are in place.

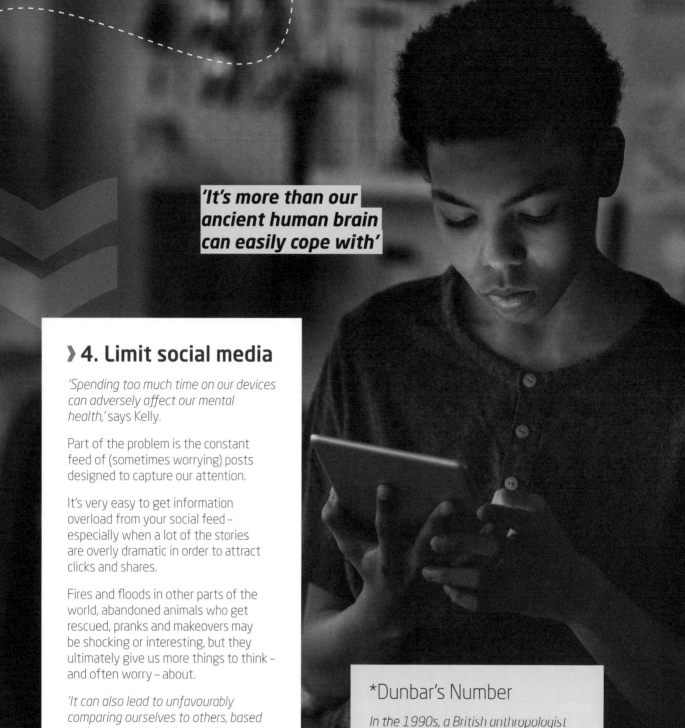

'It's more than our ancient human brain can easily cope with'

❯ 4. Limit social media

'Spending too much time on our devices can adversely affect our mental health,' says Kelly.

Part of the problem is the constant feed of (sometimes worrying) posts designed to capture our attention.

It's very easy to get information overload from your social feed – especially when a lot of the stories are overly dramatic in order to attract clicks and shares.

Fires and floods in other parts of the world, abandoned animals who get rescued, pranks and makeovers may be shocking or interesting, but they ultimately give us more things to think – and often worry – about.

'It can also lead to unfavourably comparing ourselves to others, based on factors entirely divorced from reality,' says Kelly.

All this is compounded by the number of people we follow and therefore receive posts and information from – it's more than our ancient human brain can easily cope with*.

'Limit your social use to once a day,' advises Kelly. *'And remember, you can't worry about everything going on in the world – just do what you can to help where you can. That's enough.'*

*Dunbar's Number

In the 1990s, a British anthropologist called Robin Dunbar came up with a theory which became known as Dunbar's Number. This identifies the number of people an individual can maintain a stable social relationship with – and it turns out to be around 150. This is because the neocortex part of our brain which deals with these functions developed 250,000 years ago when we lived in much smaller communities. Unfortunately our brain hasn't yet caught up with our social media habit.

'Exercise stimulates the release of endorphins'

Cadets coasteering at Annual Camp 2019

❯ 5. Exercise outdoors

Any exercise will improve your mood as it stimulates the release of endorphins and serotonin in the body – which make us feel good.

'Our bodies contain everything we need to maintain mood,' says Kelly. *'We just have to access the feel-good chemicals through exercise – in particular outdoor exercise. Being in the fresh air is calming and grounding, gives us a dose of vitamin D and literally helps us get a new perspective on things.*

'Another benefit is that when we exercise we stimulate ghrelin (the "hunger hormone") which gives us an appetite. When we're hungry as a result of exercise we feel we've earned the food we eat and so get the pleasure of reward.'

❯ 6. Trust in the future

During difficult times, such as during a pandemic, it can be scary to think about the future.

'However, it's important to keep planning and thinking about life,' says Kelly. *'We are living in ever-changing times but trying not to lose sight of your place in the world is important.*

'Think about the direction you want to go in and what you want to achieve, and focus on that; try not to worry about things you can't control.

'The world is always – and has always been – changing, and every previous generation has lived through difficult times in one form or another. It's part of being human.'

Kelly is an experienced psychotherapist and counsellor who works with young people and adults in the South West of England.

Feel-good food

Ever wondered why chowing down on a stack of pancakes cheers you up? Or find yourself dipping in to the biscuit tin when you're feeling low? **Rhiannon Lambert**, founder of Rhitrition, reveals how food can boost your mood.

'You might be surprised to learn that food has a much greater effect on how we feel than we acknowledge,' says registered nutritionist Rhiannon. 'In fact, most of the time we may be unaware of how it influences us at all.'

Rhiannon starts by explaining the biological and physiological response: 'We all know we become irritable when hungry and happy when satiated. The reason for this? Survival. Both animals and humans exhibit this kind of behaviour to increase their alertness and search for food.

'However, while our innate desire for sugar may explain why we are drawn to certain foods, it doesn't explain why we may experience guilt when consuming foods [such as sweets and chocolate] that we should be physiologically drawn to.'

Clearly there is more to food and mood than just biology; it's just as much to do with psychology.

'Our psychological experiences throughout our lives can impact how we feel about food, from the reward we get for doing well, to the ice cream we eat for comfort,' says Rhiannon.

'We live in a world that teaches us to eat when we're stressed, unhappy or for comfort.

'Interestingly, research has shown that we have a tendency to overeat when we're experiencing both positive and negative emotions. This is because consuming sweet or fatty foods seems to alleviate stress.

'Another influence on our relationship with food is our surroundings,' continues Rhiannon. 'The access we have to food (such as how much it costs and what is available) can affect how it makes us feel. For example, we may experience

'A diet that promotes positive mental health is balanced and full of variety'

positive feelings when eating something that reminds us of childhood, while research has shown that our family unit, school and work all influence the food choices we make.'

So how can we use this knowledge to our benefit and boost our mood?

'While a balanced and varied diet is always going to be best in terms of our mood, evidence suggests that carbohydrate-rich meals may improve how we feel. This is because tryptophan (found in protein sources and which helps make our "happy hormone" serotonin) needs carbohydrates to help it enter the brain.'

If we're lacking key nutrients, that can also affect our mental health. Rhiannon explains: 'Deficiencies in iron, B vitamins, folate and selenium are all linked to either tiredness, weakness or incidence of feeling depressed.

'Some research has also suggested that omega-3 may help individuals suffering from depression, but more evidence is needed in this field.'

'Carbohydrate-rich meals may improve how we feel'

What's the take-away?

'A diet that promotes positive mental health is balanced and full of variety,' says Rhiannon.

'Reach for complex carbohydrates like whole grains, a range of protein sources, healthy fats, two portions of oily fish a week and, most importantly, a colourful range of fruit and vegetables.'

Rhiannon is one of the UK's leading registered nutritionists (RNutr), founder of private clinic Rhitrition on London's Harley Street, and author of *Re-Nourish: A Simple Way To Eat Well*. She's also a Level 3 personal trainer.

Army Cadets in
Lockdown

To Inspire To Achieve

Cadets rise to the challenge

On 23 March, in a televised speech to the nation, Prime Minister Boris Johnson revealed to the public new rules to limit the spread of Covid-19 in the community. This became known as 'lockdown'.

The rules soon dominated everyone's daily life: people were told to stay home, except for limited reasons including food shopping, once-a-day exercise, and work (if absolutely necessary).

All non-essential shops shut, events were cancelled and gatherings of more than two people were prohibited. Those who did go outside were urged to keep two metres apart.

In such extraordinary circumstances, cadets relied upon values such as courage, discipline and selfless commitment to come up with new and ingenious ways to help others, continue their training and stay well – both mentally and physically – during the three long months of lockdown. Here is a snapshot of what went on.

Virtual training begins

Face-to-face cadet activity was suspended from 17 March, but that didn't signal the end of training.

Virtual training was rolled out online to all cadets to keep them occupied, help them revise their theory and, in many cases, further their progress.

Online parade nights

During lockdown some cadets took part in online parade nights. Captain Feltham of Angus and Dundee Battalion hosted a lesson on fire control orders with an interactive session which included comments and live polls.

Victory gardens

During the Second World War those on the home front grew victory gardens to ease food shortages and boost morale. While at home, cadets were encouraged to start their own vegetable gardens using everything from windowsill pots to tucked-away garden plots. Tips and progress were shared on social media.

Instagram takeover

On 24 March cadets witnessed the first Army Cadets Instagram takeover. Kickstarting the first live broadcast was adventurer and Cadet Ambassador Jordan Wylie who answered cadets' questions. It was the first of a series of Tuesday takeovers during lockdown.

Big Phil's Big Shout-Out

Army Cadet Champion 'Big Phil' Campion kept spirits high among the cadets and CFAVs with a weekly social media shoutout. He mentioned cadets and CFAVs who'd gone above and beyond.

Cadet 3D-prints PPE

Finding he had a little extra time on his hands due to lockdown, 15-year-old Cheshire ACF **Cadet Christopher Johnson** (pictured) decided to use it productively to help NHS staff.

Using his own 3D printer, Christopher started making protective face shields which could be used by frontline workers such as his aunt Joanne Eccles MBE, a senior nurse at Royal Preston Hospital (and Deputy Commandant of Lancashire ACF).

To help cover costs of materials, and in order to produce more shields, Christopher set up a GoFundMe page with the aim of raising £500. The target was quickly smashed to over £4,000.

Christopher said: *'I'm overwhelmed by the response; everyone has been so generous. We've exceeded the original goal, enabling me to purchase another 3D printer which I'll donate to a local school once this is over.'*

He added: *'I don't deserve all the accolades and praise. I'm just trying to do whatever I can to help out during these challenging times.'*

Deputy Commander Cadets Brigadier Mark Christie OBE (in post at the time) said: *'What Christopher did was truly incredible. At a time when many other young people his age might be struggling to find things to do, he used his time and skills to help those working hard to protect us. His efforts to do good and help others was something we see time and again within the Army Cadets and he must be applauded for going above and beyond.'*

After hearing about the project, National Honorary Colonel Lorraine Kelly invited Christopher and his aunt Joanne onto her TV show via Skype.

» Cadets in action

Thirteen-year-old cadet **Amitie Jo Rigby** (pictured) of Southport Detachment set up a self-service warm drinks station outside her family home so that emergency service workers didn't have to pay to get hot beverages.

Two 16-year-old cadets **Captain Danika McGowan** and **Captain Bo Anderson** (pictured) from Limavady organised an online quiz to raise money for PPE at North West Care Home.

Captain Anderson said: *'When we thought up the idea it seemed pretty simple but, once we started, it just got bigger and bigger and the support we got was brilliant.'* They raised over £200.

Lance Corporal Rowan Laws of D (Company) Dunoon Detachment was awarded the Commandant's Coin for his piping during lockdown. His recordings were used for VE and VJ Day and he also piped for NHS staff.

Cadets and CFAVs from the **Peninsula Detachment** (G Company) came together to collect and donate food and essential supplies to local foodbanks during the difficult times of lockdown.

Sergeant Sarah Jacobs of Hereford and Worcester ACF designed and produced 'Smile Masks' (made so the mouth is fully visible with a see-through sheet) for the deaf and hard of hearing community.

Cullybackey cadets (pictured) were personally thanked by the Mid and East Antrim Mayor, Peter Johnston, for their fabulous community work during lockdown. With ex-cadet Anna Henry, they assisted Cullybackey Community Partnership in making up food parcels and delivering them to the vulnerable within the village.

A stitch in time

Sixteen-year-old **Cadet Corporal Rosie Nelson** of A Company's Malton Detachment made good use of lockdown by creating face masks for family, friends and neighbours.

'One of my nannas was a Queen's Nurse and worked in the NHS for 44 years,' said Rosie. *'She actually retired a month before the Covid-19 outbreak in the UK and was on holiday in New Zealand when the global pandemic was declared. She felt she had to do her bit, so she obtained a New Zealand work visa and now tests people for the virus over there. In the UK, my other nanna is a General Nurse at a local hospice and my mum is a nurse on maternity leave.*

'I'm grateful that my family members are involved in the NHS because it gave me an insight into their – and their co-workers' – struggles. Watching their coworkers tackle the problems without the right PPE made me want to help, so that's why I decided to start making and donating masks.'

Cadet Cpl Nelson also encouraged cadets, CFAVs and parents to find out if any of their local care services needed homemade PPE and shared instructions on how to make masks.

From formula one to frontline kit

Before lockdown, former cadet **Sam Zarych** (pictured top right) of Bedfordshire and Hertfordshire ACF started an engineering apprenticeship with the Mercedes Formula One HPP Team at Brixworth.

However, with racing at a standstill due to Covid-19, the team (including Sam) turned their technical skills to building and delivering new continuous positive airway pressure (CPAP) breathing machines for hospitals around the UK.

The machines helped Covid-19 patients with lung infections breathe more easily when an oxygen mask alone was insufficient.

CPAP devices had been in short supply in UK hospitals, and the engineers at University College London and Mercedes-AMG HPP worked around the clock to reverse-engineer a device that could be manufactured rapidly.

Sam and team succeeded – and also shared the blueprints required to make the device so other manufacturers could join them in the fight against the virus.

» Taking shelter

Dorset **Cadet Ben Hall** built a replica Anderson shelter in his garden and pledged to sleep in it every night until he returned to school in September, to raise money for a local charity.

Fourteen-year-old Ben was inspired to fundraise for Dorset and Somerset Air Ambulance when, as a result of two people being saved at his local beach, he discovered each helicopter rescue costs £3,000.

Acting Detachment Commander Captain Wheatley said: *'Cadet Hall is an inspirational young man who gave up his comfy bed for the shelter in aid of a fantastic charity. A superb example of selfless commitment: one of the key values and standards of the Army Cadet Force.'*

Healthcare hero

Community spirit

Cadet Kyle McBride of the 1st Irish Guards Cadet Platoon, Crosby, put his lockdown time to good use by encouraging his community to donate essential items which he then distributed to vulnerable people.

The idea sprang from a conversation Kyle had with an elderly neighbour. When Kyle discovered that the gentleman was struggling in lockdown as he didn't have a fridge in which to store food, he took to social media (with the help of his mum) to source one. Two days later Kyle had located a fridge which was delivered to his neighbour.

Cadet Sergeant Aiden Daniel of Dyfed and Glamorgan ACF joined the frontline battle against Covid-19 when he began training to become a Health Care Support Worker (HCSW).

The 16-year-old cadet from Seven Sisters in South Wales was due to continue his studies at Afan College but instead started training with the Swansea Bay University Health Board.

'I've always wanted to give back to the National Health Service,' said Aiden. *'I had a big operation at the age of nine and spent six weeks in hospital. I admired all the staff who looked after me.*

'I've always wanted to work as a physiotherapist. I decided to apply for the role

of HCSW as I really enjoyed the placement I had in a hospital through the Army Nursing Cadet Scheme.'

The RCN Prince of Wales Nursing Cadet Scheme gives young members of uniformed organisations an introduction to potential careers in nursing.

Aiden received praise from Professor Donna Mead OBE, one of the most influential nurses of the last 70 years. She said: *'It is rewarding to see young students like Aiden wanting to get involved. He's an incredible young man and I have no doubt has a very bright future within the health sector.'*

Concerned there were other vulnerable people in the Crosby area in similar situations, Kyle started checking on elderly neighbours and using social media to ask people to donate essential items. He quickly found himself inundated with food, clothing, toiletries and toys, which he distributed to those in need.

Cadet McBride became a local hero and received letters and words of thanks, as well as a Deputy Commander's Coin medal. His mother was especially proud, saying she could overlook the fact that their living room became *'McBride's sorting office'.*

Saluting the
NHS

A cacophony of claps and cheers became a familiar sound across the nation on Thursday evenings in lockdown as the public thanked the NHS and other key workers for their dedication.

Cadets across the UK also took the opportunity to mark their appreciation with a national salute for NHS and key workers. Regimental Sergeant Major, Austin Butler, Yorkshire (North and West) ACF said at the time:

Cadet LCpl Clayton from Mirfield ACF

'As you are all aware, the NHS is working tirelessly to save lives. Your turnout for the salute must be of the highest standard – remember, you represent not only Yorkshire (N&W) ACF but also our affiliated regiments and corps. Demonstrate our gratitude to the NHS and other key workers – get on parade at your front doors and remember our values.'

The salute was massively popular with a very high turnout from the ACF.

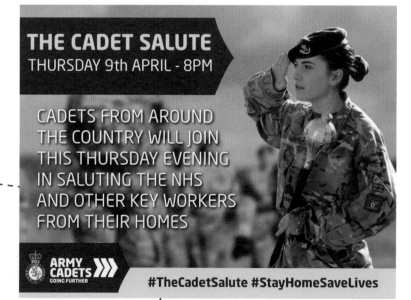

THE CADET SALUTE
THURSDAY 9th APRIL - 8PM

CADETS FROM AROUND THE COUNTRY WILL JOIN THIS THURSDAY EVENING IN SALUTING THE NHS AND OTHER KEY WORKERS FROM THEIR HOMES

ARMY CADETS GOING FURTHER

#TheCadetSalute #StayHomeSaveLives

To Inspire To Achieve

Jack and Sam climb Pen y Fan - indoors

Despite being in lockdown, two Welsh cadets stayed active by undertaking physical challenges at home.

Sixteen-year-old cadets **Jack Beynon** of 53 Wales and West Signals Squadron, Ty Llewellyn Detachment Dyfed and Glamorgan ACF, and **Sam Davies** of 104th Regiment Royal Artillery, Raglan barracks Newport, Gwent and Powys, took up gruelling but unique challenges.

'We decided to do physical challenges to raise money for Cancer Research after my sister Jade was diagnosed in early 2020', says Jack. *'We began by shaving our heads as a sign of solidarity, as she began to lose her hair due to chemotherapy.*

'We'd also planned numerous physical challenges on Brecon over the summer. However, this was affected by the Covid-19 outbreak and we were unable to train outdoors as we intended.'

Instead the pair created alternative challenges which they could do indoors. Jack explained: *'We walked the equivalent of Pen y Fan on the stairs wearing 25lbs bergens, and we completed 100 push-ups and 100 sit-ups each day for the remainder of lockdown.'*

Sam said: *'We knew these challenges would be difficult, but that's precisely why we wished to complete them; the struggle of carrying a loaded pack up a mountain doesn't compare with living with cancer.'*

The cadets raised more than £3,700 for Cancer Research UK.

Little bags of hope

Fifteen-year-old cadet **Lance Corporal Ewan Baillie** used lockdown to create 'little bags of hope' for local key workers in his hometown of Berwick-upon-Tweed, an activity he was able to use for his Duke of Edinburgh's Silver Award Volunteering section.

Ewan designed square keyrings and handmade angels which he put into voile bags. The gifts were warmly received and Ewan was sent letters of thanks from both Her Majesty The Queen and the Prime Minister's office.

DofE in lockdown

The pandemic didn't deter cadets from pursuing their Duke of Edinburgh's Awards; instead they found new and ingenious ways to complete their various sections.

Major Dan Tebay, national DofE advisor, was amazed at the sheer variety of activities cadets managed to undertake at a time when the nation was largely confined to home quarters.

'The physical challenges cadets put themselves through and the enormous number of skills learnt was truly inspirational,' he said. *'If this is the quality of future generations then we are in safe hands.'*

Read on to discover a few of the activities cadets undertook ...

Lance Corporal Jessica Sully, 15, also donned her sporting gear each day to take part in the 80km walk/run for her Silver Physical and Skill sections. She also took part in A Company Challenge completing 99 miles (the total distance between the ten detachments in A Company), helping to raise more than £250 for ABF The Soldiers' Charity.

» Devon ACF

Cadets in Devon pounded parks and pavements to take part in a virtual 80km walk/run set up by SMI Mark Sanders to help them achieve their DofE awards. These included **Lance Corporal Owen Sharmen**, 15, who not only completed his Bronze award during lockdown, but also enrolled in his Silver and played a part in raising £602 for Children's Hospice South West.

Cambridgeshire ACF

Sixteen-year-old **Kate Bilclough** kept working towards her DofE Physical by joining in with ACF county sports challenges. She used the Strava app to track her runs and walks and, by planning routes in the shape of letters, spelt the phrase Armed Forces Day (a challenge set by the country sports officer in support of Armed Forces Day).

Kate completed the 1,000 Mile Challenge, the Virtual One-Mile Challenge, Climb Mount Everest Challenge, Cycling to Cyprus and the One Million Step Challenge.

Lothian and Borders ACF

Fifteen-year-old twins **Caitlin and Leigh-Ann Lawrie** had to think on their feet as to how to continue working towards their Bronze Awards during lockdown.

Lance Corporal Caitlin had been volunteering for a Scottish charity that supports people with Cystic Fibrosis so, when she could no longer collect cans and pack bags, she started to promote the organisation online.

After sustaining an injury, Leigh-Ann swapped her usual rugby union for home circuits for her Physical. She also noticed some of her fellow cadets were not engaging with virtual training so she took them under her wing, choosing Coaching and Leadership for her Volunteering section.

'With my sports injury and then lockdown it was difficult to complete my Physical section,' said Leigh-Ann. 'However, I was able to change my activity and do exercises at home which got me stronger and then I even managed to complete Bronze level and start my Silver level.'

Sussex ACF

Lance Bombardier Harmony Lavallee, 16, completed her Volunteering section for Gold by helping to homeschool her younger siblings Takarra, 11, and Benjamin, 9, and teaching them how to bake.

» 2nd Northern Ireland Bn ACF

Throughout lockdown **Cadet Sergeant Gemma Conn**, 17, volunteered with the Drumbo Area Action Committee as part of its Covid-19 response. Tasks included delivering leaflets, distributing boxes and packing gift boxes.

'One distribution involved 70 children's activity packs containing things like colouring pencils and plenty of sweets,' said Gemma. *'As part of our community role I also helped collect prescriptions and even got a pair of glasses for a man who was shielding.'*

» Dorset ACF

Emily Graves, 16, from Dorchester detachment continued her DofE Bronze by teaching Japanese to her mum, Louise, a frontline worker and nurse.

Due to Louise's shifts at Dorchester Hospital this often meant squeezing in a lesson at 6am.

'It allowed us to spend precious time together while giving Mum the opportunity to learn something new. And I wanted to help her during that difficult time,' said Emily.

'I now have a better understanding of a teacher's perspective: a lot of time goes into making lesson plans as well as being able to make others understand them.'

Louise has vowed to continue the lessons and the family hope to travel to Japan one day to put their language skills into practice.

Merseyside ACF

Finlay Mason, 14, teamed up with a couple of four-legged friends, Teddy and Dave, to complete his Bronze.

'For my Volunteering I walked two dogs for my friend Jayne who has Parkinson's disease and is unable to walk them herself – I was really glad to help her look after her dogs,' he said.

Other news in March

Major Boris Spence retired

Major Boris Spence retired after more than 50 years in uniform. The Cadet Executive Officer spent 22 years as a member of the ACF Permanent Support Staff, although his military journey started as an Army Cadet in Blyth before he enlisted in the Army (junior service) in 1969. He spent the best part of three decades serving in the Royal Regiment of Fusiliers, before he retired to join the ACF, initially with Durham and then Northumbria, where he steadied the ship for 20 years.

Exercise Rolling Thunder

Tests in signalling and associated military skills challenged hundreds of ACF cadets at Exercise Rolling Thunder. The tenth cadet CIS competition was held on 6-8 March (pre-lockdown). Sussex Army Cadet Force were the overall winners and the Argyll and Sunderland Highlanders Battalion ACF were awarded the Pugh Memorial Trophy for Endeavour.

Jordan Wylie ran in ice-solation

Cadet Ambassador Jordan Wylie had been due to fly to the North Pole to run a marathon to raise money for Frontline Children in March, but coronavirus scuppered his plans. Determined to go ahead in some form, Jordan completed the gruelling five-hour run while experiencing the same temperature conditions as the North Pole – but in a CryoAction chamber, housed at CryoLabs Poole. *'Running in a small box for hours is really tough, especially at -33 degrees,'* he said.

» 1st Northern Ireland Bn ACF

Sergeant Tamzin McNeilly, 16, not only received her Silver DofE during lockdown, she then progressed to Gold by getting out her sewing machine and making dog bedding for rescue animals at Mid Antrim Animal Sanctuary.

'I loved the challenge of thinking outside the box for my Volunteering, not only making use of my time during lockdown but also benefiting the homeless animals in my area,' she said.

SKILL UP

Up for learning a new language or how to code or cook? Read on for ways to grow your list of accomplishments, polish your drill skills and gain new qualifications ...

8 NEW SKILLS
to learn from home

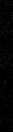

Find yourself spending too much time scrolling through social media? Put your spare time to good use and develop some new skills. You don't even need to leave the house.

1. Join
the coding crew

Dream of being a cyber engineer, computer game designer or website developer? You don't need to be at university to learn the coding basics or improve your skills.

Even if you're not planning on becoming a professional programmer, foundation-level skills will be useful in a future that's going to be thoroughly tech-focused.

A great place to start is **Codeacademy** which has a free version of its interactive programme (including an app). Take the quiz to identify which areas you're most interested in, then get stuck in.

2. History on
your headphones

From bake-alongs and TV-show debriefs to TED Talks and rugby commentary, there's a podcast for every interest.

Whether you listen to them on the move or plug in to help you drift off to sleep, podcasts are a great way to improve your breadth of knowledge.

If history is your idea of a snooze-fest, *BBC Radio 4*'s *You're Dead to Me* podcast may just change your mind. Described as 'a history podcast for people who don't like history', the entertaining series, hosted by *Horrible Histories* historian Greg Jenner, reveals fascinating facts about those historic events you really ought to know about, but don't.

3.

Sharpen your knife skills

Ready to develop some essential culinary life skills? You don't need any experience to make a tasty and inexpensive supper.

The **BBC Good Food** website has a collection of recipes – from easy-peasy stir fries to crowd-pleasing curries – designed specifically for teenagers and newbie cooks.

4.

Learn to speak Klingon

Sure, learning French, Spanish or Italian might be helpful in real life, but can they get you next-level intel (without reading the captions) on your latest binge-watch series?

Language-learning app **DuoLingo** has launched courses in TV faves High Valyrian and Klingon, so *Game of Thrones* fans can channel their inner Mother of Dragons, while Trekkies can be ready for the Klingon invasion.

DuoLingo's game-like interactive app makes learning light-hearted, while quick sessions mean you can practise for as little as a couple of minutes a day.

5. Brush up your first aid

First aid skills are always good to have and, as you never know when they'll be required, keeping them up to date is important.

Whether you're starting with the basics or want to improve your existing knowledge, an excellent resource is **St John Ambulance**. Its website is filled with helpful information, advice and tips, and covers everything from broken bones to breathing problems. You can even watch injury-specific videos on the steps you should take as a first aider.

6.

Become a genealogy detective

Exploring your family history can be an illuminating experience, revealing unknown facts about long-lost relatives and the places they came from.

Genealogy websites such as **Ancestry** and **My Heritage** have free trials so you can trace your ancestors without shelling out.

A good place to start is by talking to older relatives to get their parents' and grandparents' names so you have something to work with. Be warned: once you begin building a family tree, it's addictive.

Edit like a pro

From Instagram vlogs to YouTube tutorials and TikTok, video content is everywhere. Knowing how to create slick films isn't only fun, it could also be a valuable addition to your CV.

Most smartphones have movie editing software such as **iMovie** for iPhones, while free apps such as **Enlight Videoleap** add emojis and green-screen effects.

YouTube is brimming with tutorials covering the basics, or dive right in and learn as you go.

7.

8.

Sign up for DofE

Need some external encouragement? The **Duke of Edinburgh's Award** is a great springboard for tackling new skills – and you get a mentor who acts as your personal motivator.

Completing a Duke of Edinburgh's Award isn't about being the best at something; it's about setting personal goals and pushing

boundaries, and one of the great things about the programme is that you can personalise it to what most interests you.

There are hundreds of activities to choose from in the Skills section, including website design, snail farming, navigation, canoe building and taxidermy. Find out more at www.dofe.org and turn to page 114 to get inspiration from other cadets who are working towards their awards.

SUPERCHARGE
your skills

» The lowdown

CVQO is an education charity and learning provider which accredits the skills developed at youth organisations such as ACF.

Often fully funded (meaning there's no direct cost to the learner), CVQO qualifications focus on developing skills such as leadership, management, communication, teamwork and public service.

The accessible courses are an ideal accompaniment to cadets' school or college studies, and having these qualifications on your CV makes you stand out when applying for further education courses and jobs.

During the 19/20 academic year, over 4,000 ACF cadets gained a CVQO qualification, while nearly 500 CFAVs completed an adult award. Many of these will progress on to the next level of award.

CVQO helps young people get formal accreditation for the skills learnt at Army Cadets, helping them stand out to future employers, colleges and universities. Two cadets share their experiences.

Laura Panter

Leicestershire, Northamptonshire and Rutland ACF

'I signed up for the CVQO BTEC Level 2 qualification during annual camp 2019. I knew I would be leaving the ACF the following year due to ageing out, so I thought I would try and take advantage of as many opportunities as I could before I left.

'I was already completing my A Level studies from home, so had started to get accustomed to working independently. I enjoyed working on the booklets for the qualification because they were interesting and also offered a good contrast to my A Level work.

'I aspire to join the Police Force through its degree apprenticeship scheme, which is very competitive. The CVQO BTEC Level 2 qualification will be important when putting my application together and help me to stand out.

'I felt a real sense of accomplishment when I finished the course because it was nice to do something productive and independent during lockdown which would also benefit me in the future.

'I am so grateful to the ACF and CVQO for providing me with this opportunity – it was a lovely way to finish my experience with the Cadets.'

Finley Marston-Smith

Lincolnshire ACF

'I signed up for the CVQO BTEC Level 2 qualification because I thought it sounded like a great way to earn a practical and useful qualification. I enjoyed working through the course during lockdown. It gave me something productive to focus my energy on and will definitely help me secure employment in the future.

> **'Completing the BTEC via the e-workbook was simple and easy to do'**

'Completing the BTEC via the e-workbook was simple and easy to do: a lot of people prefer typing or don't have neat handwriting and this solves both of those problems.

'E-workbooks are easier and quicker to receive. You get emailed the relevant workbook when it's needed rather than having to wait for it to be posted, or to get together in a group to complete them. You don't have to waste paper by printing anything out, either – you just fill it in on your computer and email it back.

'The qualification will also be useful when I go back to Army Cadets as it helped me reflect on skills I already had but didn't always use or show.'

Drill skills 101

Get your drill skills polished to perfection using this step-by-step guide to basic drill manoeuvres.

One of the core skills every cadet should have under their belt is how to perform basic foot drill, which is the ability to move quickly in formation from one place to another in a formal parade.

Drill is all about self-discipline and it teaches cadets how to work effectively in a group. It also engenders a sense of pride.

As experienced cadets know, drill isn't easy to master; it requires a lot of attention and coordination in order to march, turn and salute in sync.

After the art of the drill has been conquered by a cadet, they move on to learn how to drill with a rifle.

⌃ Stand easy into stood at ease

Stand with your feet shoulder-width apart and arms bent behind your back, resting your right hand over the left. Your body should be relaxed but with a straight back.

Move into the 'stood at ease' position by forcing your arms and hands downward past your back, while raising your chin and pushing your shoulders back.

To Inspire To Achieve

» Stood at ease into attention

Lift your left knee in front of your body and bend it so your thigh is parallel to the ground and your foot hangs naturally below the knee, then promptly force your left foot down besides your right foot.

Swiftly move your arms at the same time so they are straight and against the sides of your body.

« Halt into right turn

Move at a 90-degree angle to your right by pivoting on your right heel and left toe.

Then lift your left knee in front of your body and bend it so your thigh is parallel to the ground and your foot hangs naturally below the knee. Push down quickly so your feet are together.

» Halt into left turn

Move at a 90-degree angle to your left by pivoting on your left heel and right toe.

Then lift your right knee in front of your body and bend it so your thigh is parallel to the ground and your foot hangs naturally below the knee. Push down quickly so your feet are together.

» Halt into about turn

Move at a 180-degree angle to the right by pivoting on your right heel and left toe. Then lift your left knee in front of your body and bend it so your thigh is parallel to the ground and your foot hangs naturally below the knee.

Promptly push your left foot down so your feet are together, and resume the position of attention.

« Halt into salute

Raise your right arm (keeping fingers and thumb together and palm facing the front) to your side and bend your elbow so the tip of your forefinger is one inch above your right eye.

Promptly push your elbow and hand forward and curl your fingers and thumb into a fist as you move your arm back to the side of your body.

» Marching and halting in quick time

On the command 'quick march', step with your left foot and simultaneously lift your right arm so it is level with your shoulder, push your left arm back as far as possible and keep your fingers clenched with your knuckles facing outward. Repeat on the other side of your body as you move forward.

The command 'halt' is given as your left heel strikes the ground. From this command, take a further 30-inch pace with your right foot (while alternating your arms as before) and push your left foot forward by 15 inches.

Lift your right knee in front of your body and push it back down so your feet are together. Keep arms tightly against the sides of your body.

We are

CVQO

Turning Army Cadet Force skills into life skills

CVQO is a UK education charity and learning provider. We deliver vocational qualifications to Army Cadets and their adult instructors. Our qualifications are accredited by Pearson BTEC, ILM and City & Guilds.

To find out more information or to send us an enquiry, visit our website www.cvqo.org

Earn your CVQO BADGES

BTEC L1 | ILM L2 | BTEC L2 | ILM L3

Follow us on

www.cvqo.org

ARMY CADETS GOING FURTHER

CVQO Ltd. Charity Registered in England & Wales No. 1115234. Scotland No. SC039261. Company Registered in England & Wales No. 5736932

Virtual activity boosts morale

In the absence of face-to-face training, cadets, CFAVs, ambassadors, champions and supporters pulled together online to raise morale and provide a sense of togetherness.

There was the **April Fools' post** suggesting cadets were about to get a rather quirky mobile refreshment van for fieldcraft exercises (if only ...).

Then, to encourage cadets to stay active at home, National Ambassador **Sally Orange** shared daily motivational videos via the ACF social media channels. Each day she also set a task for followers, such as thinking of ten things to be grateful for.

Another highlight was the series of **Tuesday Night Instagram Takeovers** in which ambassadors, adventurers and friends of Army Cadets did a series of live Q&A sessions online with cadets.

Takeover stars included RAF POW veteran John Nichol (right) Garrison Sergeant Major AJ Stokes (pictured with Her Royal Highness The Duchess of Cambridge), Lance Corporal Fern Davies, Medical Supply Specialist with the Royal Logistics Corps and Commonwealth Games netball athlete (below, right), and the first blind runner to complete the 7-Marathon challenge, Dave Heeley (below, middle).

© MoD Crown Copyright

First Army Cadets digi-mag launched

Undeterred by the limitations of lockdown, the plan to relaunch *Army Cadet Magazine* quickly switched from print to online, and a digital edition of April's *Army Cadet Magazine* was published ahead of the scheduled print edition.

As an online-only publication it reached tens of thousands of cadets and CFAVs across the UK, and the magazine was able to provide support, advice, entertainment and inspiration.

The emphasis was on helping cadets stay lively in lockdown by learning new skills and finding ways to occupy themselves at home, and the interactive digital format linked to video, podcasts and virtual tours.

The April issue was followed by editions in May, June, August, October and December and will continue in the same format throughout 2021.

Find back issues of the magazine on the Army Cadets website.

ACFA Hardship Relief Fund

Concerned about the impact of lockdown on the lives of CFAVs, the ACFA launched the Hardship Relief Fund.

The ACFA initially allocated £60k to the fund, and CFAVs from across the detachments were able to apply for grants. It quickly became clear the original sum would be insufficient; by the end of the scheme £200k was allocated, with 220 CFAVs receiving grants ranging from £200-£2,500.

@ Haraala Hamilton/DK

» Chris Bavin gets cadets planting and cooking

TV chef Chris Bavin inspired cadets and volunteers to get out in the garden by sharing his top tips for growing plants from seed on the ACF YouTube channel.

Later in lockdown, Chris also shared simple recipe videos for cadets to follow at home, including easy-peasy hash browns.

Pebbles for Bergen-Belsen

Throughout the month, cadets across the counties painted stones to commemorate the 75th anniversary of the liberation of the Bergen-Belsen concentration camp by British and Canadian Armed Forces on 15 April 1945.

The stones will be displayed at a new UK Holocaust Memorial and Learning Centre which is due to open in Victoria Tower Gardens near Parliament in 2021.

We'll meet again

The Eldessouky sisters of Northumbria ACF went viral in April when a video of them performing Makaton (a language programme which uses signs alongside speech and symbols) to We'll Meet Again by Vera Lynn was aired on ITV's *Lorraine*. The sisters learnt Makaton as part of their DofE skills.

Royal helping hand

Army Cadet volunteers helping to distribute care packages at Frimley Park Hospital were given a royal helping hand by Her Royal Highness The Countess of Wessex in April.

The Countess, who lives close to the hospital, helped volunteers package food and care parcels which were given to NHS staff.

FOOD

Read on for camp cooking ideas, and the ultimate pizza and doughball recipes for Friday night fake-aways. Plus, we quiz nutritionist Rhiannon Lambert on how to eat healthily on a budget.

Camp cookout

Camp food doesn't have to be all bangers and beans. Rustle up these cookout crowd-pleasers and find yourself elevated to head camp-chef status.

» Campfire cooking safety tips

1 Make sure you have the landowner's permission to build a fire and only do so away from overhanging branches, dry grass or anything that may enable a fire to spread.

2 Keep the fire small enough to put out if needed – have water, sand or earth on hand to extinguish it.

3 Make sure the fire is fully extinguished with water before leaving (using earth alone can leave smouldering embers).

4 As on a barbecue, cook over hot embers rather than flames.

5 Use a frying pan suitable for a campfire and cook in the same way you would over gas or an electric ring.

6 Be aware that pan handles will get hot, so use a mitt or cloth when picking them up.

7 Creating skewers from sticks? Be aware the wood will burn. Soaking in water first will help.

8 Food cooked in foil should be placed in the cooler embers at the edge of the campfire.

CAMP PANCAKES

Make sure you've got happy (and full) campers by treating them to fireside pancakes oozing with maple syrup and topped with fruit.

❯ Equipment

Frying pan

Spatula

❯ Ingredients (serves 2)

Plain flour 150g

Salt 1 tsp

Cinnamon 1 tsp

Egg 1, beaten

Milk 240ml

Melted butter 1 tbsp, plus a little for cooking

Maple syrup to serve

Fruit to serve

❯ Method

Prepare the dry ingredients and the wet ingredients in two separate jars at home. Then, when you're ready to make your pancakes, pour the wet ingredients into the dry ingredients and shake up the jar.

To cook, add a little butter to the pan, pour in some of the pancake batter and cook for a couple of minutes over hot embers. Turn the pancake over when it's golden on the bottom, then repeat on the other side.

Repeat with the remaining batter.

Serve with maple syrup and fruit.

BANANA BOATS

Bananas will replenish energy levels and can be turned from a simple piece of fruit into a scrummy dessert.

Cut a slit in the banana's skin and flesh, poke in a few pieces of chocolate and marshmallow (you can add biscuit too to give you something to scoop the gooey filling out with), then foil-wrap and cook for 10-15 minutes in the campfire embers.

S'MORES

S'mores means "some more" and when you try them you'll understand how they got their name.

An American camp favourite, s'mores are easy to make – with ingredients that won't suffer from being carried in a rucksack.

Toast a marshmallow on a stick until it turns golden brown, then sandwich it with a square of chocolate between two biscuits. The American classic uses Graham Crackers, which are not that easy to get hold of here, but digestive biscuits work well.

Go next level by adding a dollop of crunchy peanut butter to the sandwich and, if you want to make them really melty, wrap individual s'mores in foil and leave them right on the edge of the embers for a few minutes.

'Go next level by adding a dollop of crunchy peanut butter'

ULTIMATE HOT CHOCOLATE

The smooth molten deliciousness of this rich hot chocolate will be a big hit on chilly nights.

❯ Equipment

Saucepan

Mugs

❯ Ingredients (serves 4)

Milk 600ml

Double cream 140ml

Chopped chocolate or chocolate buttons 100g

Whipped cream for topping

Mini marshmallows for topping

Grated chocolate for topping

❯ Method

Pour the milk, double cream and chopped chocolate into a saucepan.

Bring the mixture to a gentle boil over the embers. Remove from the heat and stir until smooth, then serve in mugs.

Top with whipped cream, mini marshmallows and grated chocolate.

fake-away

Use this basic recipe for both pizza and doughballs.

Why splash out on takeaway pizza and doughballs when they're so easy to make?

❯ Ingredients

Egg 1, lightly beaten

Sugar (any kind) 2 tsp

Yeast (20g fresh or 10g dried)

Yogurt (plain or greek) 4 tbsp

Vegetable oil 3 tbsp

Milk 170ml

Bread flour (also called strong white flour) 400g

Salt 1 tsp

❯ Method

1. **To make the dough:** lightly beat the egg in a large bowl (if you are making the dough in an electric mixer use its large bowl).

2. Add the sugar, yeast, yogurt and vegetable oil. Stir to combine. Warm the milk and add to the other ingredients.

3. Add the flour and salt and mix everything together to form a dough.

4. **To knead the dough:** if you're going to use a machine to do the kneading, fix the bowl and dough hook in place and turn the machine on medium speed for 5 minutes until the ingredients have formed a silky dough.

5. If you're going to knead the dough by hand, turn it out onto a clean worktop which has been lightly dusted with flour. Knead for 10 minutes.

6. **Let the dough rise:** put the dough back in the bowl and cover with a damp tea towel or clingfilm and leave in a warm place for a couple of hours.

MAKE DOUGHBALLS

1. Follow steps 1 to 6 left, then lightly oil 3 large baking sheets.

2. Cut the risen dough into 34 pieces. Place on the baking sheets, cover with damp tea towels and leave to rise again for 20 minutes.

3. After 15 minutes, turn the oven to 240°c / gas 9.

4. The doughballs will cook best in small batches, one baking sheet at a time. Cook in the oven until they are golden in colour and sound hollow when tapped on the bottom. Repeat.

5. Serve with garlic butter (mix a crushed garlic clove with a pinch of salt and 100g softened butter).

If you want a thinner crust, stretch the dough so it's as thin as possible.

MAKE PIZZA

1. Follow steps 1 to 6 (far left) to make the dough, then turn the oven to its highest setting.

2. Lightly oil a large baking sheet.

3. Place the risen dough on a clean, lightly floured worktop and cut it into quarters.

4. Put 3 pieces aside and work on your first pizza base. Gently push out the dough with your fingers to make a circle. You could use a rolling pin, but the dough tends to stick to it. Better to lift the dough and gently pull it in different directions, letting its weight stretch it out as you turn it.

5. When you've created the size of pizza base you'd like, place it on the baking tray.

6. Dress the dough with tomato sauce (make your own by cooking down a can of chopped tomatoes, half a finely chopped onion, a splash of olive oil, a couple of crushed garlic cloves and a pinch of salt). Then add cheese and whatever toppings you like.

7. Cook the pizza in the oven until it's crisp, puffed up and bubbling (make the next while the first is in the oven).

How to eat healthily
(on a budget)

Want to give your body good-quality fuel without running up a massive shopping bill? Nutritious food needn't be expensive if you know the tips and tricks, reveals **Rhiannon Lambert**.

Utilise your freezer

'Frozen fruit and vegetables are not only cheaper, they can also have a higher vitamin content than fresh alternatives. This is because the fresh variety can lose vitamins during transportation and storage, while freezing immediately preserves them.

'Try defrosting blueberries in the microwave to make a sweet sauce to drizzle on porridge, or throw a handful of frozen peas into a curry.'

Try tinned

'Just like frozen foods, tinned ingredients are cost-effective and have a long shelf life.

'Versatile tinned foods I like to have in my cupboard include chickpeas, beans, lentils and tomatoes. With a little imagination a few tins can easily make a meal: how about rustling up a kidney bean chilli or lentil cottage pie?

'It's also worth remembering that vegetarian protein sources like pulses and legumes contain fibre, and diets rich in fibre are linked to a reduced risk of heart disease, diabetes and colorectal cancer.'

Make the most of dairy

'While there are certain dietary requirements and choices that result in people avoiding dairy, it is good to note that it's a rich source of protein, calcium, iodine, phosphorus and B12.

'The nutrients in dairy products help support muscle and bone health, growth and brain development, as well as the immune system. Dairy products are very useful in cooking as they can be used as a key ingredient in many dishes.

'Try to limit consumption of dairy items high in saturated fat such as hard cheese; instead choose items like milk and natural yogurt.

'If you drink dairy alternatives instead of milk, check they're fortified with essential vitamins and minerals including iodine, vitamin B12 and vitamin D.'

Spice instead of salt

'We all need to eat less salt: it's estimated that the average adult consumes over two and a half times the recommended 6g per day.

'Even if you're used to adding salt to dishes for flavour, you'll find that food can still be tasty without it. Spices and herbs such as coriander, cumin, turmeric, basil and paprika are an effective way of making food taste good without adding lots of salt.

'Spices have a long shelf life as long as you keep the packages airtight. Look for them in the world-food section of the supermarket.'

'Defrost blueberries in the microwave to make a sweet sauce to drizzle on porridge'

Rhiannon is one of the UK's leading registered nutritionists (RNutr), founder of private clinic Rhitrition on London's Harley Street, and author of *Re-Nourish: A Simple Way To Eat Well.* She's also a Level 3 personal trainer.

© Tamin Jones

Army Cadets in
May 2020

Taking on the challenge of mental-health awareness

To mark Mental Health Awareness Week on 18-24 May, members of the Army Cadet family – including Army Cadet Ambassadors Jordan Wylie (pictured) and Sally Orange, Army Cadet Champion 'Big Phil' Campion and Captain Alison Campbell – shared a series of personal audio messages with cadets via social media. Themes included the participants' own experiences of mental health challenges, and what kindness means to them.

Virtual pat on the back for DofE Gold Award holders

This year's DofE Gold Award holders couldn't attend presentation ceremonies at St James' Palace and Buckingham Palace in March and May, so His Royal Highness The Earl of Wessex (pictured) shared a special message of congratulations via YouTube.

The Earl recognised the dedication and hard work required to achieve a Gold Award, and was joined in the congratulatory message by a host of famous faces including Levison Wood, Aldo Kane, Judy Murray and Gaby Roslin.

VE Day celebrations

While the Army Cadets' celebrations to mark the 75th anniversary of Victory in Europe Day couldn't go ahead on 8 May in the same way as planned, detachments across the country still joined forces (virtually) to celebrate.

Band together

One great highlight of the day was the virtual band of cadets and CFAVs (pictured). Each recorded themselves playing the same medley of wartime songs in their own homes, and when the music of the entire band was played together it sounded incredible. The talented group was also featured on ITV's *Lorraine*. Big thanks to 2nd Lieutenant Kate Knight for editing the footage.

Walking the walk

Determined to get outdoors in some form or another, Cambrai Company asked its detachments to walk a total of 75 miles while adhering to social distancing rules. Four detachments completed the challenge and covered an impressive 300 miles, raising £460 for the charity Frontline Children.

The Company also hosted a VE Day-themed Operation Cake competition.

Great British Bunting

Thanks to all the cadets and CFAVs who got involved in *BBC Radio England*'s Great British Bunting campaign. The colourful flag chains decorating windows and houses across the country on VE Day were spectacular to see.

KIT

We love good kit: it helps us perform better, is a pleasure to use and, just occasionally, survival depends on it. Read on to find out what we couldn't do without ... and what we'd love to own.

Kit we couldn't do without ...

We asked a few experts and instructors to reveal their favourite kit and why it's important to them.

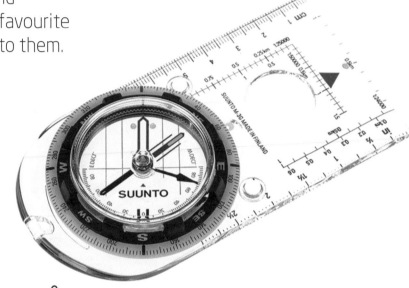

William (Ginge) Morris,
Navigation Advisor,
160 Welsh Brigade ACF

SUUNTO COMPASS

As ACF Mountain Leader and Navigation Officer for Wales, Ginge recently assisted in writing the Army Proficiency Certificate (APC) Navigation syllabus, so he certainly knows a thing or two about how to use a compass – indeed, it's the one thing he'd never be without.

'You could be the greatest soldier in the world but if you can't get to where you need to be ...'

'A Suunto compass is my instrument of choice,' he says.

'Everyone thinks a compass is just for navigation but that's not the case. You can tell the time using one (in coordination with the sun), it's got a magnifying glass on it so you can look in fine detail on the map, you can use the magnification to start a fire, and the compass contains a means of measuring.

'Basically, most of the things we do on the APC syllabus require a compass: fieldcraft needs one for navigation and rangework needs one to work out angles for firing templates. I don't feel equipped if I don't have one on me.

'You could be the greatest soldier in the world but if you can't get to where you need to be, it's a bit pointless,' he says.

Major Andy Toze,
OC Adult Training,
Hampshire and Isle
of Wight ACF

SNUGPAK SOFTIE 3 MERLIN SLEEPING BAG

'For years I used standard issue kit in which the sleeping bag would take up 90 per cent of the space in my Bergen,' he says.

'Then, on recommendation, I invested about £65 (a fair amount of money ten years ago) in a Snugpak Softie 3 Merlin sleeping bag. It was the first large-scale kit purchase I made and it was a game changer.

'It was so light I found I could move faster when carrying my Bergen and, because it fits in the palm of one hand when scrunched up, my Bergen was a lot less bulky.

'As it's so small I often take it in my day pack as a backup. It's been useful on Dartmoor and in the Brecon Beacons when the weather has closed in; I've been really glad to have it with me.

'It's warm and robust and, when used with a bivvy bag, is a brilliant piece of kit.'

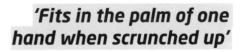

'Fits in the palm of one hand when scrunched up'

BLIZZARD 3-LAYER SURVIVAL JACKET

Andrew Lester,
Adventurous Training
Development Manager,
Army Cadets

'It doesn't matter what I'm doing – whether in the mountains climbing, in my kayak paddling whitewater, or ski touring – I take one of these with me as they're potential life savers. And they're so small they easily fit in the bottom of my rucksack or back of my boat,' Andrew says.

'You can send it to Blizzard afterwards and they'll repack it'

'It's a great piece of emergency kit that's essentially a glorified silver blanket. But instead of being a bag, it's a jacket, which gives you the big advantage of still being able to move.

'They are made from three layers of Reflexcell™ material – heavy-duty silver foil to you and me – and are lightweight. I think they're pretty cheap at around £33.

'Fortunately, I've never had to use it "in anger", but if you do you can send it to Blizzard afterwards and they'll repack it for you, so it's not a one-hit wonder.

'Mountain rescue teams use them and sing their praises. Blizzard also provides thermal equipment for the military.'

CRUSADER METAL MUG

SLEEPING-BAG LINER / INFLATABLE PILLOW

Mark Jones, Sergeant Major Instructor, Army Cadets

'In the military we have a 58 Pattern water bottle that's been with us since 1958 and which has a plastic cup. The cup often breaks, and I've also found that cadets tend to put them on cookers and accidentally melt them, so they're not great.

'When you're out in the field, not only do you need your water bottle, you also need mess tins to cook food in – and carrying both takes up room. However, in the 1940s the Army produced a 44 Pattern bottle and mug which were both metal. People used to cook, boil water and drink tea from the same mug, which saved space – and washing up.'

'It's a really simple piece of kit which lightens your load'

Mark decided to follow the lead of those earlier soldiers and, 18 years ago, bought himself a metal mug which he's taken with him on trips to Gibraltar, Germany, Afghanistan and all around the UK.

'It's a really simple piece of kit which lightens your load and does the job. I've shaved out of one, drunk tea out of one – and, at the very least (some say), you can dig with it.'

Liz Green, Major, DofE Development Manager, Army Cadets

'These are relatively low-cost items which enable you to have a good night's sleep on expeditions – which makes a big difference to your performance.

'Many cadets borrow sleeping bags from the stores but having their own liner makes it a more personal item and also adds excellent insulation. You can pull it up inside your bag for extra warmth or, if you get too hot when the sun shines on your tent in the morning, you can peel back the bag and still have cover and privacy.

'They pack down small and make sleeping out much more comfortable'

'I bought my sleeping-bag liner when I was doing my Mountain Leader assessment; I knew I was going to be the only female in the group and therefore be on my own in a tent (so likely to get cold). I bought a silk liner – you can get them in cotton and fleece too – and was very grateful to have it so I was warm during the night, slept well, and felt refreshed the next day.

'I'd also recommend getting an inflatable pillow – I have one with a fleece cover – as they pack down small and make sleeping out much more comfortable.'

... and kit we'd like

We asked some members of the Army Cadet family what they'd like to own.

SSI Ross Wheeler-Clayton,
Detachment Commander of Parkstone, Dorset (ACF)

SNUGPAK STRATOSPHERE BIVVI SHELTER

'Since seeing a fellow DofE Assessor on a Silver Expedition using the Snugpak Stratosphere Bivvi Shelter, it's been on my wish list.

'The one-person tent weighs 1.3kg and measures only 31cm in the bag. It's lightweight and compact, making it incredible for expeditions.

'This piece of kit stands well against the harsh weather while keeping the user warm for a more enjoyable experience.'

DANNER BOOTS

Colonel Clint Riley (ACF)

'I would be pleased to receive a pair of Danner boots.

'In the early 2000s I had several pairs (prior to the Army issuing better footwear) and they're hardwearing and comfortable. Since then I have used the issued boot – but if a pair of these were available I would be tempted.'

To Inspire To Achieve

MACWET CLIMATEC LONG GLOVES

BLACK LEATHERMAN WAVE+

Brigadier Stuart Williams OBE, Deputy Commander Cadets

The Brigadier chose a pair of MacWet Climatec Long Gloves for their *'all grip and no slip'* functionality.

'They're superb when handling weapons of all types,' he asserts.

The water-resistant Climatec glove range was developed to protect hands in cooler weather, keeping them warm through wind-proofing and the use of fleece-lined material on the back of the glove. Unique Aquatec® fabric ensures grip and sensitivity – and they even come in a choice of colours.

Colonel Anthony Lamb
MBE VR DL, Colonel Cadets (CCF Army)

'It would have to be a black Leatherman Wave+ laser engraved with "Lambo" (sorry, couldn't resist) and in matt black so you can't be seen deploying it (or be able to find it in the dark).

'You never know when you'll need one: your sleeping bag zip gets stuck, barbed wire needs to be cut between you and your objective, a pesky tick needs extraction, your dried biltong needs slicing, you need to adjust your rear sight in the hope of hitting your target on the range at 300m, or your baked beans can loses its ring pull … '

AG600 SEAPLANE

Army Cadet Ambassador and polar explorer, Craig Mathieson

'If it's in the realms of fantasy, it has to be an AG600 – the world's biggest seaplane.

'This piece of kit can hold 50 passengers and has a range of around 2,700 miles. I'd base it in the UK and use it to fly Polar Academy and ACF Expedition teams to the most remote places on Earth, for an adventure of a lifetime.'

Know your WEAPON

BSA Scorpion Air Rifle Cadet Sporter .177"
BSA Scorpion Air Rifle Cadet .177"

Two variants of this weapon system have been developed to meet the needs of the British Military Cadet Force. They're used for training and competitions, and are the first weapons cadets will be taught to use in the Skill at Arms syllabus.

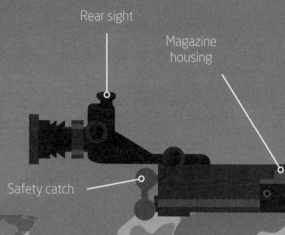

Rear sight

Magazine housing

Safety catch

Butt

Bolt and bolt handle

Trigger and guard

Two of a kind

Both of the weapons are simple to learn and operate. They're robust, and a good cleaning and maintenance regime will ensure they rarely become inoperable. The air rifles can be used on indoor ranges at 5.2m and outdoor ranges at 10m.

What's the difference?

The BSA Scorpion Air Rifle Cadet .177" is a single shot weapon system, while the BSA Scorpion Air Rifle Cadet Sporter .177" has a multi-shot capability and can be fitted with a ten-round magazine or a single-shot adaptor.

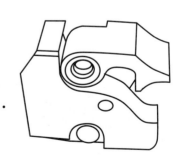

Single-shot adapter

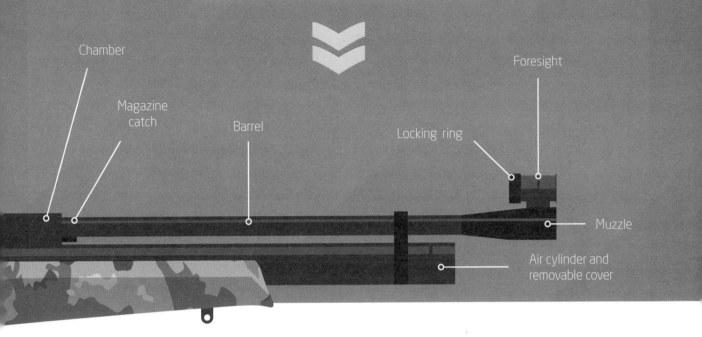

BSA Scorpion Air Rifle Cadet Sporter .177"

Chamber

Magazine catch

Barrel

Locking ring

Foresight

Muzzle

Air cylinder and removable cover

Sighting system

- The weapons are fitted with highly accurate front and rear dioptre sights.

- The sighting system has a fixed foresight and can be adjusted for elevation and direction by adjustment screws.

- To move sights up for elevation, turn the adjustment screw located at the top of the sight clockwise, and to move down turn anti-clockwise.

- To move the sight laterally to the right, turn the directional adjustment screw located at the right side of the rear sight clockwise; to move the sight laterally to the left, turn it anti-clockwise.

Air pressure

This is pre-charged into a fitted air cylinder using a Hills Hand Pump and can be monitored and kept maintained at a usable pressure by a trained CFAV.

Positioning

Both air rifles can be fired from standing, kneeling and prone firing positions.

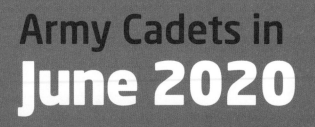

Virtual Armed Forces Day

Armed Forces Day (27 June) was a little different this year. Instead of the usual colourful parades and activities by which the Army Cadets joins the nation in showing its support for the men and women who make up the armed forces community, the celebration was creatively reimagined.

Live performances, a Red Arrows flypast and a message from Her Majesty The Queen took place, while thousands visited the Armed Forces Day website and social channels to celebrate, and learn about, the work of the armed forces.

Socially distanced celebrations by the public included themed quizzes, barbecues and picnics, which were shared online using #ArmedForcesDay. Many also paid tribute by posting photographs of them saluting, using #SaluteOurForces.

Lincolnshire ACF on a more normal Armed Forces Day in a previous year

Captain Carrie
Whareham
IOM ACF

One-mile heroes

Army Cadet Sports organised a virtual one-mile running competition in June. The event was open to all cadets and CFAVs who were tasked with running a mile – as quickly as possible – within their local area.

The runners uploaded their results to an online competition tracking tool and, to beat their previous PB, ran as many times as they wanted.

Over 1,000 runners took part and National Sports Development Manager Terry Hayter said: '*The aim was to give cadets and CFAVs an opportunity to participate in a challenge and provide a focus towards fitness, and physical and mental wellbeing. The event also helped them feel more connected within the Army Cadet family.*'

Participants were awarded a National Competitor badge and those who reached podium positions in their age group were awarded a medal.

Northern Ireland and Canadian cadets unite

To commemorate the 76th anniversary of the D-day landings, the Royal Canadian Army Cadets and Northern Ireland Battalion ACF met for the first time – via Zoom.

The Act of Remembrance and the playing of the Last Post was followed by a session in which Canadian DSM Kutchew, Cadet CSM Carrie Morrow of Glengormley Detachment, and Under Officer Paige Abernathy of Ballymena Detachment explained the roles of the Canadian and British troops on D-Day.

Afterwards, cadets and instructors joined a quiz hosted by Canadian RSM Dumais, before splitting into different virtual chats to get to know each another.

Corporal Matthew Marron from Ballyclare Detachment who, before lockdown, had been going through the process of Canadian Cadet Exchange said: '*We hope to remain in contact with our Canadian friends and someday get the chance to meet.*'

Pride at CTC Frimley Park

Sadly, lockdown put a stop to the fantastic Pride parades and street parties held each year in support of the LGBTQ+ community. However, we took great pleasure in showing our support by lighting up CTC Frimley Park at the beginning of June.

Cadet gets chance to shine

Christchurch cadet Grace Taylor (pictured with Jordan Wylie) won our Ambassador's creative writing competition in June, and was presented with a new paddleboard by Jordan. She said: *'One of the fantastic things about being part of Army Cadets is that it's not only the sporty types or loudest cadets who get recognised – we all have a chance to shine.'*

Century of celebrations

To mark the 100th anniversary of the formation of The Royal Corps of Signals on 28 June 1920, cap-badged Signals from Yorkshire (North and West) ACF detachment took part in a series of national events.

These included participating in #100for100, a fitness challenge where a detachment works together to amass a total of 100km by walking, running or cycling. The Corps of Signals awarded a special plaque to each Signals cap-badged detachment that achieved the 100km goal.

At B Company's Strensall Detachment, Detachment Commander Lt Mike Richardson (pictured) and 2IC SSI Charlie Henson spent the month inspiring their cadets to complete the 100km challenge, which led to B Company's Officer Commanding Major Rory Romani joining in the fun, too. The activity resulted in the detachment receiving a plaque.

Game to win

At the start of lockdown we launched a writing competition asking cadets to tell us why their detachment is special.

We received 700 entries, and in August revealed the four cadets who won the money-can't-buy prize of having their name and detachment immortalised in the new **Monopoly: Army Cadets Edition** board game.

For this new version of the classic game, the team at Cadets HQ worked with the gamesmiths at Monopoly to introduce berets, boots and mess tins in place of the Scottie dog, top hat and battleship. Property squares were renamed after camp locations, and the board changed so players now build lecture rooms and training blocks instead of houses and hotels.

What makes this even more special, however, is that the four train stations on the board have been named after the four competition winners' detachments. The winners' names are printed on the back of the board and their detachments received a 'deed card' plaque to display.

Congratulations to Leah Flett, Alliyah Evans, Jodie Place and Eden Armstrong who all received a *Monopoly: Army Cadets Edition* board for their detachment.

It was inspiring to read the entries, and choosing just four was extremely difficult. Here are the best bits from the winning entries:

Alliyah Evans
14th Platoon, Berkshire ACF

14th Platoon gave me a place where I felt I belonged, and I am proud to be a part of it.

The 14th Platoon are the best because they welcome you, no matter who you are.

I've made true friends and I feel more confident in myself – at school I'm now known as "The Cadet".

Jodie Place
Thornaby Detachment, Cleveland ACF

When I first started Cadets I was shy and a troublemaker at school.

I used to wander the streets causing mayhem but after joining the Cadets I gained confidence and am now able to make new friends in a group of strangers – and I've stopped getting into trouble. My parents describe me as a completely different child.

Going to Cadets brought me closer to my family and out of my shell.

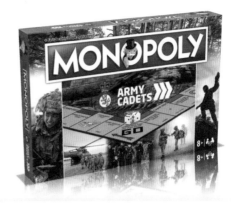

Eden Armstrong
Christchurch Detachment, Dorset ACF

So many people show their commitment to the detachment. The adult volunteers, our DC, the NCOs and cadets all work together selflessly, giving time and effort to each other.

Our detachment is always respectful. Whether it's a visitor, a friend from school, a parent or the DC, respect is given willingly and this reflects back to us.

Leaving the detachment is a sad thought for anyone, yet our detachment imparts a strong impression of loyalty to anyone who does leave.

In our detachment we adhere to strong morals and principles. Our integrity is what makes us so popular with new cadets and why they want to join. You'll find no bullying here.

Duties are performed to the best of our abilities. Attention to detail is given to our uniforms, parade and even running the NAAFI. As a unit, discipline is expected and we all strive to achieve it.

Sgt Leah Flett
Annan Detachment, West Lowland Battalion

Two nights out of my week I go,
to a place that makes my cheeks glow.
I walk suited and booted through the door,
and see my friends and family that I adore.

The family atmosphere at Annan is what I love.
Cadets come in and are sent achieving above . . .
And beyond what they would ever believe themselves to.
This is because we support one another to pull through.

New Army Cadet diversity and inclusivity role

In July we were delighted to announce Major Darren Hughes' appointment as the Army Cadet Force's first National Diversity and Inclusivity Adviser.

Darren was promoted to Lieutenant Colonel and, in the new national volunteer role, will work on the ACF Step Change Diversity and Inclusion Project. He will also lead a network of volunteer Regional Diversity and Inclusivity Advisers.

The advisers look for new ways to increase awareness of diversity and inclusivity at all levels, and have a mission to celebrate, educate and recognise the diverse nature of the organisation.

Darren said: '*I'm exceptionally proud to have been appointed the ACF's first ever National Diversity and Inclusivity Adviser.*

'*Having been the Bde Cdt D&I Adviser for 51 Infantry Brigade in Scotland for the past ten months, I look forward to working with the ACF family across the UK to strengthen our resolve and take forward the great work already undertaken by the ACF Step Change team.*

'*I will stop at nothing to embed inclusion and diversity into the core of our great organisation.*'

FIRST AID

Courageous cadets demonstrate first aid skills

A group of Merseyside cadets put their first aid training into action (pictured) at the beginning of July. They encountered an elderly man in Sefton Park who had experienced an unprovoked attack and needed immediate assistance for significant injuries.

The young cadets assessed the situation, called the emergency services and administered first aid.

After they asked for the gentleman's permission to check his injuries, they assessed a bleeding laceration above his eye and a large cut on the back of his head. They used their first aid training (and initiative) to stem the bleeding using a nappy they sourced from a passing woman with a baby.

The cadets reassured the shocked man and kept passers-by from overcrowding him as they waited for the police and ambulance to arrive.

The young people's actions were widely praised by the media. LCpl Bella Lowe, 16, said: *'It sounds strange, but we didn't think of it as a big deal; we were just helping an old man who needed help.'*

ACF Merseyside Commanding Officer Major Edgerton said: *'Merseyside Army Cadet Force is honoured to have such mature and thoughtful youngsters within our youth group.'*

In the same month, 15-year-old LCpl Amy Lindsley from Harraby Detachment used her first aid skills to help an injured neighbour.

After hearing shouting in the street and spotting a woman lying on the ground, Amy ran to the scene and quickly took control of the situation, placing the neighbour in the recovery position and reassuring her until an ambulance arrived.

Cadet Lucy Feighery, from Rochdale Detachment of Greater Manchester ACF, shaved her hair off for the charity Chelsea's Angels – which supports families with children diagnosed with cancer – and raised over £750.

Sharman Birtles, JP DL, Honorary Colonel of Greater Manchester ACF said: *'I am extremely proud of being Honorary Colonel and never more so than when I hear of wonderful young people such as Lucy. She is the epitome of what the Army Cadet Force is all about.'*

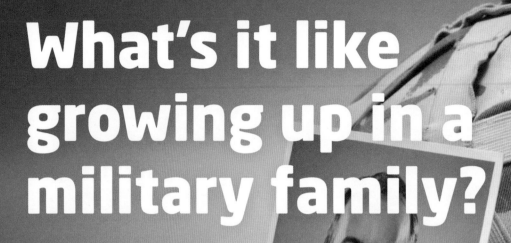

What's it like growing up in a military family?

Six cadets from across the counties share their experiences of growing up in military families – and reveal how it's shaped them and their plans for the future.

Joseph Carroll, 14

Heaton Detachment, Northumbria ACF

'Growing up in a military family (my dad, mum and older brother are all in the Army Reserves) gives you a different perspective on life.

'My parents have taught me the importance of keeping fit: I train regularly in the gym and as a family we've completed the Great North Run several times to raise money for ABF The Soldiers' Charity, a cause we're all passionate about.

'Having a good routine is another life skill I've learnt from them and I've also been taught about the importance of military history – it's proved quite useful at school.

'I've been a cadet for three years and it's been a great way to make new friends, learn new skills and do fun stuff like shooting competitions. I'm definitely going to follow in my family's footsteps and join the Army Reserves when I'm old enough.'

'I've been taught about military history - it's proved useful at school'

'I've lived in more places than I can remember'

Hannah Hopkins, 15

Bedworth Detachment, Warwickshire and West Midlands ACF

'My dad, a regimental sergeant major, recently left the Army after 23 years in the Royal Signals.

'I've lived in more places than I can remember as his job has moved us around the UK, but it's been a great way to meet new people and I've made some lifelong friends.

'Living on barracks introduced me to other children whose parents were serving in the military and it was comforting to speak to others who knew how I felt when my dad was away on tour. It was tough not being able to speak to him every day.

'The experience has taught me to be quite independent: my siblings and I had to do a lot of things for ourselves. Moving from school to school has also made me confident about speaking to new people.

'I definitely want to join the forces in the future – I'd like to be an officer in the Medics. My dad has always been very supportive and encouraged me to go on to bigger and better things than him; I'd like to do a degree before I join.'

Harvey Stone, 17

Rossett Detachment, Clwyd and Gwynedd ACF

'My parents met in Portsmouth when my mum was a Navy nurse and my dad was in the Army in the Royal Electrical and Mechanical Engineers (REME). Although my mum retired when I was born and my dad passed away when I was one, I feel our family and friends have instilled a military mindset in me. For example, I know if you want to do something it's you who has to put in the work – no one else is going to do it for you.

'I've been told lots of stories about my dad's time in the Army and he's inspired me to also join the REME – I'm going through the application process at the moment and it's both exciting and nerve-racking. My friends and family have told me tales – good and bad – which have helped me know what to expect.

'I've had a lot of friends who've left because their families are in the military'

'While I've never had to move around, I've had a lot of friends who've left because their families are in the military and that was really tough. When I have a family in the future, I'm not sure I'd want to bring up children on a camp or make them move away from their friends.'

Amelia Sinclair, 14

Limavady Detachment, 1st (Northern Ireland) Battalion ACF

'There are positives and negatives to growing up in a military family. My dad's job (as a WO2 in the Royal Logistic Corps) meant we moved every two years to a new country or a new area, which was hard. I had to make new friends and it was difficult to keep in contact with the ones I left behind.

'When we moved to Northern Ireland I had to keep my dad's job secret'

'When Dad was away on deployment we'd often spend time with my family in Germany, which made the experience easier. When we moved to Northern Ireland I had to keep my dad's job secret and that was tough.

'However, it's been great to experience living in different places. We've been in Northern Ireland for five years now and I feel really settled. I joined the Cadets two years ago and it's been a great way of making new friends and learning life skills.

'I'm definitely leaning towards a career in the military, although I wouldn't want to be on the frontline – I'd rather do something with radio.

'I'm very proud to be part of a military family and get a great sense of pride when I wear my Cadet uniform on Armed Forces Day and Remembrance Sunday.'

Dafydd Ashton, 17

Bovington and Purbeck Detachment, Dorset ACF

'Growing up in a military family ingrains certain attitudes and teaches helpful life skills you may not acquire in a non-military family. My dad (who is a WO2 with The Royal Welsh Regiment) taught me the importance of routine and how to present myself by ironing my clothes, maintaining good posture and using good manners. I know how to hold myself in difficult situations.

'I've always wanted to go into the Army (I've been a cadet for five years) and being able to talk to my dad about his experiences has given me an insight – I think it can be a shock for people who join without any prior knowledge. I've lived on camps which, at times, was quite isolating as there weren't many children my age, but now I know what to expect if I live on one again. Being part of the Cadets has shown me different routes my career in the Army could take.'

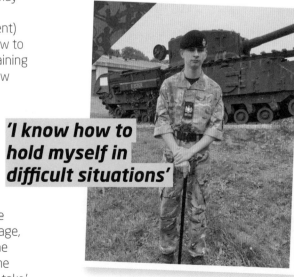

'I know how to hold myself in difficult situations'

Ashlynne Downie, 14

Cottingham Detachment, Humberside and South Yorkshire ACF

'Both my parents have a military background: my dad was in the REME until 2013 (he's now in the Reserves) and my mum was in Phase 2 training when she became pregnant with my sister.

'Growing up in a military family teaches you to look at things more logically'

'I've lost count of the number of places we've lived as, when I was younger, we moved quite regularly. We'd often live on barracks with other families where there were lots of children my age, so it was easy to make friends; it felt like a proper community.

'In 2008 my dad was deployed to Afghanistan for seven months and that was really tough for us, especially my mum who had just had my little sister. We couldn't call him but we were able to send letters which we did as regularly as possible to keep his spirits up.

'Growing up in a military family teaches you to look at things more logically – in school I often observe how someone is doing something and question why they would go about it in that way.

'I've known for a long time I'd like to join the military as a vet – I prefer animals to people – and my parents are really supportive.'

CFAV saves man with suspected knife wound

Second Lieutenant Scott Baker of Yorkshire North and West ACF was awarded a Meritorious First Aid Award for his quick actions in August which potentially saved a man's life.

The CFAV's first-aid training kicked in when he helped a man with a suspected knife wound. Twenty-two-year-old Scott was socialising with friends in Hull city centre when he came across a man who was sitting in a pool of blood and surrounded by bar and security staff outside a pub.

Scott identified himself as a first aider and took charge by confirming with security staff that an ambulance had been called. He set about stemming a major bleed from the man's wrist and elevating the joint.

With the bleed under control, Scott confirmed the casualty was not in possession of a bladed article and checked there were no other significant visible injuries.

When the man started showing symptoms of shock and became unresponsive, Scott was able to move him into an improvised recovery position, keeping the injured joint elevated and directing a bystander to elevate the man's legs.

Scott continued to monitor the casualty who drifted in and out of consciousness. A passing police patrol took stock that the incident was under control and remained at the scene to help disperse onlookers.

When paramedics arrived, Scott gave them a full verbal handover and assisted the ambulance crew in getting the casualty onto a stretcher while maintaining pressure to the wound.

His quick actions earned him praise from his Officer Commanding, Major Romani, who said: '*2Lt Baker epitomises the dedication of our volunteers to help those in need. His ACF first-aid training probably saved the man's life.*'

County STEM Officer Scott said he was able to help because he had rehearsed similar scenarios during training: '*After nine years of first-aid training in the ACF – as both a cadet and CFAV – I was well prepared to deal with the situation.*'

Summer camps go virtual

During August cadets camped out in the garden and at home

With annual summer camps cancelled across the UK, some counties, such as Essex ACF, took to the internet to host a virtual camp.

During the two-week Essex ACF Virtual Annual Camp, cadets participated in activities from their homes – although that didn't mean standards were relaxed; everyone attended in uniform.

Lessons included first-aid sessions where SSI Gene Morris showed cadets novel ways to create realistic injuries using things found in the home: PVA glue and talcum powder for blisters, Alka-Seltzer and water for acid burns, face paint for bruises, and corn syrup with food colouring for blood.

Many took part in The Commandant's Big Camp Out where Commandant Colonel Leona Barr-Jones (pictured) challenged everyone to camp out. Cadets (and, in some cases, family members) enthusiastically pitched tents, bashas and improvised shelters. Some cadets and CFAVs chose to make the experience even more like a regular summer camp by cooking outside.

In total, 425 cadets, parents and adults took part in 50 sessions on Zoom, and challenges included a virtual cross-country run, a fieldcraft quiz and lessons on skill at arms and cooking in the field.

On the final day of the camp, the Commandant awarded trophies and gave the results of the virtual Annual Camp Competitions, naming D Coy as the overall winner.

Cadet Sergeant Stacey Thrower from Leigh-on-Sea detachment, C Coy, was awarded a special prize for her winning T-shirt design which featured a tent, computer screen and depiction of a Zoom lesson.

The Commandant rounded up the camp, saying: *'I want all adults and senior cadets to know they have been a role model and an inspiration to all the cadets who have been with us over the last two weeks. The cadets have all achieved great things – some more than they ever thought was possible – and the instructors have put them on the road to becoming the best that they can be.'*

Hidden history

The Stock Exchange Cadets

When **Sergeant Major Instructor Mark Jones** discovered a treasure trove of photos and letters about a cadet unit created in the London Stock Exchange after the First World War, he made it his mission to share the incredible story it revealed.

Coming across the name Major Max Karo MBE in a book was the spark that ignited SMI Jones' interest in finding out who this name from history really was.

After much digging he found that, like himself, Major Karo had been a member of the City of London and North East Sector ACF. So he delved into the archives at the Whipps Cross Cadet Centre and found long-forgotten documents that completed the puzzle of who the Major was and the part he played in forming the Stock Exchange Cadets. SMI Jones is now sharing his discovery to ensure the story isn't (once again) lost to history.

» Social climber

Max Karo, a Jewish man from Breslau, started his working life as a bank clerk in Berlin. At the age of 20, with no family to speak of, he moved to London with the company he worked for.

In Victorian London, Max worked hard and networked in order to move up in society. He would spend his weekends going for tea at Claridge's and mixing with wealthy businesspeople (many of whom he ended up working with later in life). In 1902 he was awarded British citizenship.

» World at war

At the age of 38 Max joined the Army and, along with his colleagues (as was usual in the First World War), became part of the 26th Royal Fusiliers "Bankers Battalion", and served in significant battles in France.

The War Office received a request for a Jewish regiment to be formed, initially resulting in the Zion Mule Corps and, eventually, a Jewish Legion made up of the 38th, 39th, 40th, 41st and 42nd Battalions of the Royal Fusiliers. Sergeant Max Karo agreed to transfer over as Company Sergeant Major for B Company 38th Fusiliers, where he was popular and well-respected – a natural leader. The company fought in Egypt and Palestine.

» Back to London

After the war, Maj Karo went back to London and his life as a stockbroker. However, he had been inspired by his time in the Army, and possessed a drive and dedication to serve others which he wanted to put to use.

He was soon helping the Jewish Lads Brigade, and later transferred to the Army Cadets. He had always loved sports – especially football and cricket – and became the Vice President of the Stock Exchange Football Club. Yet he saw the need for further recreation for young men in the City.

Sergeant Max Karo, 26th Royal Fusiliers.

Image from City Milestones and Memories: Sixty Five Years in and about the City of London by Max Karo, published by Weidenfeld & Nicolson

What is the stock exchange?

A system for buying and selling stocks and bonds (also known as 'securities').

Stocks are a share in the ownership of a company, and therefore a share of the company's profits, while **bonds** are an agreement to lend money to a company for a certain period of time, in exchange for being paid interest.

The **London Stock Exchange** in the City of London was set up in 1571, making it one of the oldest in the world. Other important stock exchanges are found in New York and Tokyo.

Many thanks to Pam Potts who kindly shared this image from her family's personal collection. Captain Arthur Stanley Potts, Pam's father-in-law, is pictured second in line behind Maj Karo

So, in 1926, Karo used personal contacts and family in France to help get 800 cadets to Boulogne for a summer camp.

Today that would be difficult to pull off; in the 1920s it was an extremely impressive achievement. The trip would have been one of the first times most of the cadets had left the UK, and Max was struck by their enthusiasm and enjoyment.

» The Stock Exchange Cadets

He discussed the idea of setting up a cadet unit in the Stock Exchange with Captain JC Latter, who had been tasked by the War Office with reporting back on the success of the summer camp. Capt Latter thought it was a great idea, raised it with the authorities, and approval was granted.

Within a day, a letter was sent to all firms of the Stock Exchange asking for their support – and their younger members of staff. The first drill night took

place between 6pm-8pm at a local school and 30 young men attended. The unit was established.

This was eight years after The Great War and a time of great optimism. The young men were enticed by the promise of a youth club that would give them a holiday by the sea, but also a sense of duty to King and country (which would have resonated with them after hearing war stories from their fathers and brothers).

The Stock Exchange Rifle and Revolver Club provided a place to shoot and learn marksmanship, and instructors from the Guards Division helped with drill – which led to the cadets taking part in the Lord Mayor's Procession (a privilege still undertaken today by the City of London and North East Sector Cadets).

The first camp took place in Cookham and was attended by 80 cadets, and was followed by many more in the home counties and abroad. Honours included parading in front of the French President and the Queen.

> *'Today that would be difficult to pull off; in the 1920s it was extremely impressive'*

The Stock Exchange Cadets Band at Bisley, 1928

The Stock Exchange Cadets in the 1950s under CO Major SS Scales (centre). Maj Karo is the white-haired man to his left

» Pranks and practical jokes

The Stock Exchange Cadets got up to their fair share of mischief.

At the unit's original meeting place, Drapers Hall, someone filled a polishing wheel with tea leaves which, when switched on, covered both one poor member of staff and the room in old tea leaves.

In the group's first overseas trip to France in 1937, Maj Karo allowed the cadets to order what they wanted in a cafe – from a choice of coffee, tea, milkshake or hot chocolate – only to find Cadet Gillett and three friends polishing off a bottle of Champagne. Their excuse? *'It's very, very cheap!'*

» Second World War

As the Second World War began, the Stock Exchange Cadets evolved from turning out good citizens to turning out soldiers. Maj Karo set up a voluntary course in the Stock Exchange to prepare both older veterans and young men with training in military subjects, map reading, drill, and skill at arms. A British Pathé film of this training is one of the only pieces of evidence to be found online when searching for 'Stock Exchange Cadets'.

Around 60 cadets didn't make it back from the Second World War, but those who survived formed the Stock Exchange Old Boys Association. The group held annual dinners where they'd meet with former detachment members. An impressive guest list demonstrates the unit's (and Maj Karo's) influence and connections: in 1948 three Major Generals, a General and the Chairman of Lloyds attended.

Brush with death

During The Blitz, Maj Karo visited a cafe which was so crowded and overpriced he decided to eat somewhere else instead. Within five minutes of leaving, a German bomb hit the cafe, killing 150 people. In shock, Maj Karo found himself walking down Lower Regent Street, questioning why he had been spared, when a builder's axe fell from above, brushing his clothing and hitting the ground in front of him.

After brushing with death twice in one day, Maj Karo reportedly went home and spent the next couple of days under a table.

To Inspire To Achieve

» End of the Stock Exchange Cadets

By the age of 75, Maj Karo – who in 1945 received an MBE – had served almost 25 years as commanding officer of the SEC. He was then forced to step down as the War Office decreed that no officer in the Cadets should serve beyond the age of 65. The new CO was Major SS Scales, a former Stock Exchange Cadet himself. The unit outlived Maj Karo MBE and continued until 1966 when the cadets were transferred from the Fusiliers to the Royal Green Jackets, part of the City of London and North East Sector.

The unit was considered extremely successful – the talk of the City at the time – with former members holding some of the highest positions in the Army. Yet few people today have heard of it, or the man behind it.

'What are we to make of this small man who was, on one hand, a hero of the Jewish people, having served in France and the Middle East, and on the other a youth worker who put his heart and soul into helping the youth of London and his adopted country?' asks SMI Mark Jones.

'His dedication to the ACF is beyond question, and clearly he loved the City of London. He mixed these two passions into one ... he took up arms for the King and then trained the next generation to do the same. What's so surprising is that this important figure has slipped between the cracks of history.'

Happily, through Mark's work documenting Major Max Karo's life, he's putting the injustice right.

SMI Mark Jones is involved in CFAV training and has been involved with Army Cadets since 1998. By day he's a criminal defence solicitor and he also served in Army Reserve Unit 3 Military Intelligence Battalion for a number of years.

Father figure

Maj Karo MBE was a natural role model who poured his efforts into helping others. Here's what his contemporaries said about him:

'The daddy of our company. He was patient, tolerant and kindly.' Mr Harry Comras, 38th Royal Fusiliers

'Major Karo is a bachelor and has adopted the cadets as his family ... devotes his time, labour and thoughts to them as a father might to his children.' Bystander Magazine, 4 February 1934

'Nearly everything you are, and nearly everything of value that you have done, spring from his generosity and from the immense amount of time and trouble that he takes for the sake of the corps.' Mr RP Wilkinson, Deputy Chairman of the Stock Exchange, 1940

Not only did Maj Karo use his personal funds to set up the Stock Exchange Cadets, he also bought new premises for the unit, which included an orderly and sergeant room, canteen, gym and a games room.

Obituary

'With the death of Max Karo a dynamic and colourful personality has departed from the floor of the London Stock Exchange ... He was an edifice of kindness, helpfulness, loyalty and devotion to his people and his country. His life work was the creation of the London Stock Exchange Cadets which was a brilliant success. Many of his cadets today hold some of the highest positions in the City.'

The Jewish Chronicle, 20 April 1962

Army Cadets in
September 2020

Brigadier Stuart Williams takes over as our new Deputy Commander Cadets

W e were delighted to announce Brigadier Stuart Williams OBE as our new Deputy Commander Cadets in September.

From his previous role as Assistant Chief of Staff Cadets, Brigadier Stuart was well placed to take over from Brigadier Mark Christie OBE, ensuring seamless continuity within the organisation.

Brigadier Stuart said: *'As Deputy Commander Cadets I have the great job of supporting the General in overseeing the command of Army Cadets. This new appointment is about driving forward positive change.*

'I love Army Cadets and everything it stands for – we set people up for lifelong success. It is the job I have wanted for a number of years – how lucky am I to have secured it?'

Brigadier Stuart was commissioned into the Royal Artillery in 1989. The early years of his Army career were spent on the 105mm Light Gun, as an Arctic Warfare Instructor in the Allied Command Europe Mobile Force (Land) and as an Armoured Forward Observation Officer in Germany and on the prairie in BATUS. Operational tours in Northern Ireland (Belfast)

To Inspire To Achieve

Brigadier Mark with his son Karl

and Bosnia were interspersed with appointments as a Platoon Commander at RMAS and on the staff in HQ 20th Armoured Brigade.

From 2000 to 2006 he served as a Major in Germany, in Kosovo and in the UK. He commanded J (Sidi Rezegh) Battery in 3rd Regiment Royal Horse Artillery, attended the Advanced Command and Staff Course 7, served on the staff in Headquarters 1st (UK) Armoured Division and was Second in Command of 26 Regiment RA.

On promotion to Lieutenant Colonel in 2007 he moved to Warminster as SO1 Junior Officer Tactics Division prior to commanding 3rd Regiment Royal Horse Artillery, a Germany-based Close Support Artillery Regiment, from 2009 to 2011.

'It is the job I have wanted for a number of years – how lucky am I to have secured it?'

In 2012 he deployed to Afghanistan and HQ ISAF, Kabul as the SO1 Ministerial Engagement. On promotion to Colonel, he spent time as a Divisional Director at ICSC(L) and then Assistant Chief of Staff Operations in HQ British Forces Cyprus.

The Brigadier first became involved with Army Cadets when he was Deputy Commander of 7th Infantry Brigade and Headquarters East (The Desert Rats), the role he held before becoming Assistant Chief of Staff Cadets.

... and we say goodbye to Brigadier Mark Christie

We said a sad farewell to Brigadier Mark Christie OBE after his successful 18 months as Deputy Commander Cadets – and an incredible 33-year Army career which took him all over the world.

An awesome individual and leader, Brigadier Mark was a valuable asset to the organisation. When asked to identify highlights of his time with Army Cadets, he said: *'Seeing cadets and CFAVs in action. I managed a lot of this before the pandemic and it was always a great pleasure to see how the organisation develops, inspires and gives opportunities to young people from every background.*

'Having CEP 500 successfully delivered on my watch was a particular triumph, but there were also less obvious wins, such as relationships with other organisations – which we worked hard for. Between Stuart and I, and with the support and hard work of the Branch, CTC, the CTTs and others, I believe we have put the organisation on the map with the Army, which now has a much better understanding and appreciation of the organisation it sponsors.'

As the Brigadier transitions from Army to civilian life he is exploring new employment opportunities and also reports he is *'on the verge of buying a cross-country motorbike – once my wife Clair finally agrees to it.'*

David chained to a 3kg medicine ball to highlight mental health challenges
Left: David presenting coin to Lilie-Maye

David Lightfoot becomes first Army Cadet Sergeant Major Instructor

David has long been a passionate advocate for the transformational power of the Army Cadets and credits the organisation with dramatically turning his own life around. Aged 14, after having been arrested for burglary and in trouble at school, he was sent to his local ACF by his mother.

'I was a bad lad at school and couldn't engage in lessons,' he said. 'However, the ACF completely changed the way I thought: my grades improved, my attitude improved and the way I went about things improved. It really saved my life.'

He has just completed 24 years in the Army, having worked his way up to the rank of warrant office regimental sergeant major, yet he still feels grateful that, when he was a troubled teenager all those years ago, his detachment commander believed in him.

'Some of my teachers wrote me off and the parting words from my geography teacher were: "The next time I see you, you'll be on the front of the newspaper for having committed a heinous crime".

'But I thought, No, I can do this, and decided to enrol in the Army. That's why I am passionate about the ACF because I want people to succeed in whatever they choose to do. If I can do it as a Yorkshireman who left home with no GCSEs, so can they.'

David will be familiar to many after his three-year deployment at CTC Frimley Park where he helped train CFAVs. He has fantastic memories of his time at the training centre, including a heartwarming story about a 14-year-old cadet called Lilie-Maye Knight who was due to have a muscle-lengthening procedure on her lower calf, followed by casting.

'Her mum tweeted that Lilie-Maye was worried about the operation and felt alone. I picked up on it and, in no time at all, she got messages from people right across the Cadet Force. Instead of feeling alone there were now 40 people telling her she could do it, which gave her the strength to face the operation. That's the power of the Cadet family.'

After the operation, David presented Lilie-Maye with a CTC Frimley Park coin.

David is also an advocate of shining a light on mental health challenges: he chained himself to a 3kg medicine ball for a week to highlight the anxiety, stress and depression some in the Armed Forces carry around with them as they cope with mental health problems.

'If I can do it as a Yorkshireman who left home with no GCSEs, so can they'

'The whole concept of mental health and wellbeing was a hot topic at the first ever RSMI Senior Cadets Conference at CTC Frimley,' he said. 'A cadet stood up and asked Colonel Riley and me what the ACF and CCF were doing for the mental health and wellbeing of cadets. At the time nothing was in place, so we took her point and talked to Regional Command.

'Two years later, the organisation has created the Healthy Minds Syllabus for cadets. It's so important that cadets know where to get help when things are hard and they feel they have no one to talk to. It's tougher than ever for kids; as a dad of three I want help to be there for everyone.'

David is looking forward to his new role supporting the regimental sergeant major instructors across the Cadet Force and he's impressed by the way detachments have coped during the coronavirus pandemic.

'It's forced us to be innovative, think outside the box and discover new ways of delivering training online. The CFAVs have been engaged to keep the flame alive and they, and the chain of command, have done a fantastic job.

'The Cadet Force is all about learning to be resilient. What we can say is the bad times will end and the good times will start again. Life may not return as we know it, but it will be better because we'll have discovered new ways of doing things.'

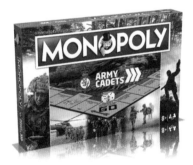

Monopoly: Army Cadets Edition

The new limited-edition Monopoly board game, designed especially for the Army Cadets, was launched in September.

Berets, boots and mess tins replaced the Scottie dog, top hat and battleship, and property squares were named after camp locations.

What made this even more special, however, was that the four train stations on the board were named after the detachments of the four winners of our summer writing competition (they also got their names printed on the back).

The board game is available from www.armycadetswebstore.com and costs £30.

Discover who won the competition on page 162.

NEW
BATTLEFRONTS

How realistic are the virtual skirmishes in online military games like Counter-Strike and Call of Duty? And how do the tactics used compare to those employed in real-life battles? We asked **Corporal Tyler Daysh**, Royal Engineer, lifelong gamer and manager of the British Army eSports Team.

'Soldiers make for very good eSports athletes because they know real-life tactics which are proven to be successful'

Developers of military games spend millions making sure their games are as realistic as possible. Everything from the noise of the gunfire to the battlefield settings are created with meticulous attention to detail. Military experts are even brought in to make sure everything looks and feels as true to life as possible.

Gamers, of course, understand that shooting games are virtual fantasies, but are there any skills and tactics that could be transferred to a real-life combat situation? We asked Corporal Daysh.

When playing a game like Counter-Strike, do you use realistic military tactics?

Absolutely! It's one of the only first-person shooters with realistic spray patterns.

In military training you're taught the four **marksmanship principles** and you have to apply them whenever you shoot a weapon.

On Counter-Strike you also have to apply marksmanship principles when shooting: you have to make sure you're not walking when you shoot or you won't be able to aim accurately.

'You have to apply marksmanship principles when shooting'

Similarly, if you don't adopt a **firing position** – crouch, lie down on the floor or stand still – the round won't go accurately.

The use of **cover** is also very similar in games to actual military encounters. You'd never pop your head up and down from the same place in real life or your enemy would just aim and wait – it's the same in a game.

Movement is comparable, too: in real life you fire and move (zigzagging so you're not running in the same line), making it harder for the enemy to aim at you. You can do the same in a game to your advantage.

To Inspire To Achieve

Above: Sergeant James Cronin and Lance Corporal Daniel Cox mentoring a young gamer

Which gaming skills would be useful to a soldier in the British Army?

〉 Hand-eye coordination

The ability to react quickly and move your hand with pinpoint accuracy is hugely important in gaming. If you focus your eyes on a crosshair on a computer screen you build muscle memory – transfer that from online gaming to shooting a rifle down a range and you're a marksman.

In my opinion, Counter-Strike is the number one competitive first-person shooter game in the world. Games such as Call of Duty, Valorant, Battlefield, Fortnite – none of them compare on a competitive level. The hand-eye coordination required to be a good Counter-Strike player is ten times that required to be a good Call of Duty player.

〉 Determination

Gamers are totally determined: they set out to complete a goal in a game and that's exactly what a soldier needs to do.

〉 Focus

Gaming requires a lot of focus and, as a soldier, you are given tasks that also need a high level of focus.

〉 Perseverance

I've been playing a game called RuneScape for 19 years and have invested a huge amount of time in it.

〉 People management

I learnt to manage personnel by being part of clans in online gaming and by organising online eSports events. The skills you learn in the gaming community are highly transferable.

In games, we use something called **slow peek** and **fast peek** which is also used in real life. When you hold a sniper rifle and slowly peek around a corner, the moment you see any part of an enemy, you fire. However, if you're using a small pistol, a submachine gun or a rifle, you quickly peek around that corner and shoot – even if someone's not there.

That's another tactic we use in real life; we call it a **pre-fire round**. Knowing you're going to shoot somewhere before having to register a target gives you a huge advantage. While the enemy still needs to mentally register what they have seen, and

'The ability to react quickly with pinpoint accuracy is hugely important'

transfer that knowledge into actual motor responses and return fire, you have already decided your shot.

Soldiers make for very good eSports athletes because they know real-life tactics that are proven to be successful and, when they apply those in a game, they work.

How did the Army get involved in eSports?

The British Army eSports team started in April 2019 off the back of an event called Insomnia 64. It runs twice a year and attracts up to 100,000 people – and is growing. There's a huge audience out there.

After seeing all those teams and eSports organisations, five of us Royal Engineers decided to create a Royal Engineers eSports Club. There are now 12 clubs in the military and 700 members of the British Army eSports Club.

What advice would you give cadets looking to develop their gaming skills?

There are a lot of events and arenas across the UK where you can play with professionals or other enthusiastic gamers.

There are also online forums where teams recruit new members. Some of them are just amateur teams but playing with a team and getting to know each other and building friendships is really good.

If you play with the same people, you learn how they react and that's just how a section in the British Army works: a seasoned infantry section won't even communicate with each other as they already know how the others are going to react to their action.

'Transfer that from online gaming to shooting a rifle down a range and you're a marksman'

If you want to learn specific tactics then YouTube is an amazing tool – there are loads of guides on it.

We've also got the British Army Lions League on Twitch TV. Keen gamers can watch live gameplay and even communicate via a chat box to the players. They can see the caster and presenter of the game, who will talk to them on camera while they're typing questions.

Tyler is a corporal in the Royal Engineers and manager of the Royal Engineers eSports Club and the British Army eSports Club. Watch him play in the Lions League on Tuesday and Thursday nights.

GO FURTHER ❯

You can watch live games on the Lions League channel on YouTube. There's a different game each evening: Monday is League of Legends, Tuesday Counter-Strike, Wednesday Call of Duty, Thursday Counter-Strike and Friday Call of Duty.

Army Cadets in
October 2020

Return to face-to-face training

Approval was given for the recommencement in October of face-to-face Army Cadet Force activities in England, and outdoor training in Scotland. This was with the proviso that the activities be conducted in accordance with the current COVID-19 guidance given by the Government or authority and Army Cadet HQ.

© Alan Walter

© Ben Stevens

» Virtual STEM camp

Following Army Cadets' successful Science, Technology, Engineering and Mathematics (STEM) camps run in previous years (pictured), we were not going to let adhering to social distancing rules stop us from holding a virtual version.

From 26-29 October, cadets across the UK got involved in interactive activities, presentations and insights into the role of STEM in the Army, delivered by a range of Corps Engagement Teams (CETs) from the Royal Signals, Intelligence Corps, Corps of Royal Engineers and many more.

Intelligence missions, challenges, quizzes and Q&As with experts demonstrated to participants the techniques used to overcome military problems. Participating cadets received the National STEM Camp Badge, a record of attendance in their Record of Service, and an Industrial Cadet Award certificate and badge from eTrust.

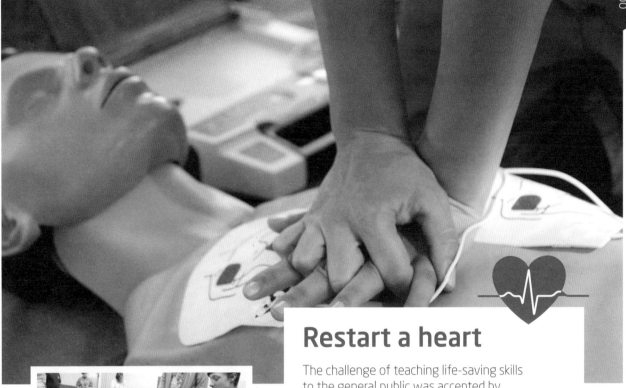

Restart a heart

The challenge of teaching life-saving skills to the general public was accepted by detachments across Clwyd and Gwynedd Army Cadets Burma Company.

Restart a Heart is an annual day of action which aims to teach cardiopulmonary resuscitation (CPR) skills to as many people as possible. From 16-23 October, staff and cadets joined international resuscitation councils from across the globe to run free demonstration sessions.

Well done to the Bangor, Penmaenmawr, Llangefni, Amlwch, Llandudno, Conwy and Holyhead detachments which held open evenings where the public could be trained in CPR and basic first aid skills.

Pictured: the Mayor of Llandudno learns how to perform CPR

Bremont Army Cadet Watch

We were delighted to launch the latest addition to Bremont's collection of highly esteemed timepieces made in partnership with the MoD: the new Bremont Army Cadet watch.

The Broadsword-style collector's item is a limited edition and available exclusively to Army Cadet members and volunteers directly linked to the organisation.

GUINNESS WORLD RECORDS
RECORD HOLDER

Deepest Underground Marathon
Distance Run (Team) | *10 October
2020, United Kingdom*

Most Users To Take An Online
Mental Health Awareness
Lesson In 24 hours | *10 October
2020, United Kingdom*

Beneath the surface

Two new Guinness World Records™ titles set in a single weekend

'Running in 30-40 degree heat in a dusty mine with minimal lighting ... for eight hours and 31 minutes'

Sally Orange and Jordan Wylie with Guinness World Records™ adjudicator Glenn Pollard at the completion of the marathon at the mine.

To mark World Mental Health Day on 10 October 2020, the Army Cadets made history by setting two new Guinness World Records™ titles.

The first was a new record for the Deepest Underground Marathon Distance Run (team) which took place at ICL Boulby Mine in north Yorkshire.

Representing the Army Cadets were Ambassadors Sally Orange and Jordan Wylie who ran the whole marathon at a minimum of 1,000 metres below ground.

'The world's deepest underground marathon'

The pair endured a demanding and punishing test of both physical and mental resilience, running in 30-40 degree heat in a dusty mine with minimal lighting and only a head torch to light the way. Their team completed the run in eight hours 31 minutes, raising money for SSAFA (the Armed Forces charity), Young Minds, and Frontline Children.

Guinness World Records™ adjudicator Glenn Pollard gives Sally Orange a socially distanced congratulatory elbow bump.

'It was a unique and gruelling challenge for all involved which really demonstrates the power of what can be achieved when you reach out to support each other – which is how poor mental health can also be managed', said Sally.

'It demonstrates the power of what can be achieved when you reach out to support each other'

The purpose behind the Beneath The Surface marathon was to highlight how hard it is to know what is going on beneath the surface in someone else's mind.

To complement the run, a second record was undertaken for the Most Users To Take An Online Mental Health Awareness Lesson in 24 Hours. The hope was that, after the course, participants would be able to recognise the signs of poor mental health and help end the stigma and discrimination surrounding it.

A whopping total of 1,622 cadets and CFAVs took part in the online course and can now proudly say their names are in the record books.

They were supported in their attempt by the Army Digital team at Field Army HQ and Defence Technology Enhanced Learning, coordinated by Neil Reeves.

Jordan Wylie and Sally Orange with Guinness World Records™ adjudicator Glenn Pollard and the official certification of the two records.

Brigadier Stuart Williams was delighted with both Guinness World Records™ achievements:

'The efforts shown by those involved in both the planning and delivery of the weekend's activities shows how important mental health is to all within the Army Cadets,' he said.

'1,622 cadets and CFAVs took part in the online course ... and now have their names in the record book'

'The importance of mental wellbeing cannot be overstated. I am in awe of our incredible ambassadors for running the underground marathon and ever grateful to our cadets and adult volunteers who took and passed the online mental health course and, by doing so, increased their understanding of this important subject.'

HEALTHY MINDS

1 in 4 people will have a mental illness at some point in their lives. It starts with gradual changes in thoughts, feelings and behaviour. Seeking help is the first step to staying well, so Army Cadets has developed **Healthy Minds** in order that cadets and CFAVs feel comfortable reaching out for support.

› How are we helping?

We aim to increase awareness, reduce stigma and promote resilience in order to support the wellbeing of cadets and CFAVs. Examples include:

- The online mental health awareness course used in the record attempt. This is now available for anyone to see what the programme is about.

- A mental health awareness course for CFAVs.

- In 2021, there will be training for CFAVs with a duty of care for other CFAVs to encourage open, non-judgemental support.

› 5 steps towards positive mental health

These steps have been shown to improve emotional and mental wellbeing:

1. Connect with others Build a sense of belonging and self-worth, share positive experiences and provide mutual emotional support.

2. Get physically active Raise your self-esteem by setting and achieving physical goals – it changes the chemicals in your brain and improves mood.

3. Learn new skills Boost your confidence and build a sense of purpose.

4. Be kind Giving to others creates a sense of reward and develops self-worth.

5. Practise mindfulness Notice your thoughts, physical feelings and the world around you.

Just how tough is Army officer training?

'I'm 5'1" and no weightlifter and I was fine: the key attributes needed are determination and perseverance'

Twenty-two-year-old ex-Army cadet **Christy Hunter** passed out from Royal Military Academy Sandhurst (RMAS) this year, earning a commission with the Royal Signals. She shares her story.

What's your background?

'I grew up in Norfolk and moved to Durham when I was 12,' says Christy. *'I ended up joining Durham ACF when I was 14 – I was quite a late joiner.*

'I didn't know anything about it really, but I was looking for something to do and found that Army Cadets was just down the road. I tried it out and I really enjoyed it. It sounds *a bit embarrassing, but I really liked the kit inspections, drills and the regimental smartness.'*

After A levels, Christy went to university to study biomedical science and, in her first year, joined the University Officers' Training Corps (UOTC*). She says: *'They push for people to go the officer route and that's the reason I applied. It suited my more relaxed leadership style – I'm not a shouty sergeant major type.'*

Although there's no obligation to join the Army after being in the UOTC, Christy decided she would apply to RMAS to undergo Army officer training and, after completing the selection process, was accepted.

'Many people are daunted by the idea of applying to be a commissioned officer,' she says, *'but it's definitely achievable.'*

Did having been an Army cadet give you an advantage in the selection process?

'Having leadership experience from being a cadet really helps with the command task elements of the process,' says Christy.

'The activities cadets get involved in can set them apart: Adventurous Training trips make great talking points in interviews and demonstrate that you've had experiences others may not have had.'

How difficult are the physical challenges of the selection process?

'It's not as physical as you'd expect. You do have to pass physical tests (including a beep test, a ball throw and a mid-thigh pull) but they are all at achievable standards. You also need to be able to show stamina and resilience on the assault course and in command tasks.

'I'm 5'1" and very petite – certainly no weightlifter – and I was fine: the key attributes needed are determination, perseverance and, when you get knocked down, cracking on with it. Those are just as important as physical fitness.'

You were one of three females among 35 officer cadets in your platoon ...

'Currently, less than 10 per cent of officer cadets at Sandhurst are female, which is a shame.

'There's a stereotype that Army officers are privately educated boys but, while 40 per cent

'The activities cadets get involved in can set them apart: Adventurous Training trips make great talking points in interviews'

of them are, 60 per cent aren't, and the Army wants a variety of backgrounds and experience.

'I was paid during the training, so it's an option for anyone. You don't need to have a degree either: you also complete academic studies at Sandhurst, so those without a degree will start working towards one (for free) while progressing their Army career. As I already had a degree I've now started a masters.'

Because Christy applied for officer training after she'd got her degree, she missed out on the bursary [grant] people can receive to help fund their studies. She says: 'If you apply and are accepted to be an officer while you're in sixth form or during your degree you can get funding while at university. That can be up to £24,000.'

Her new role with the Royal Signals will involve learning about satellite communications rather than biomedical science. She says: 'I decided not to use my degree; I realised I wasn't so interested in the subject, so I'll be learning a lot of new skills.'

And, with two years left of her three-year contract, what's the plan?

'I'm hoping to stay in [the Army] for 15 years until I reach major and have a masters and civilian-accredited qualifications under my belt.'

---

*UOTC is a university society, sponsored by the Army, where students learn military skills, make friends, travel, and learn leadership and teamwork skills.

COULD YOU HANDLE IT?

Captain Polly Marsh of Royal Military Academy Sandhurst (RMAS) reveals what every potential officer cadet should know ...

1. Expect to dig deeper than you've ever done

The training is designed to wear you down and attempts to break your spirit. You'll almost certainly fail a task or not reach the standards required at least once. It'll be frustrating; be prepared.

Officer cadets undertake a simulated casualty evacuation from the battlefield

(c) RMAS (Taken prior to social distancing)

2. Don't judge by appearance

Judge others by resilience, loyalty, integrity, team spirit, dedication and determination. RMAS training is the ultimate leveller and cadets come from all social backgrounds, cultures and religions, and are of various ages, genders and sexualities. Everyone is treated the same and, as an officer cadet, you need to be able treat everyone else in the same way.

'The power of hope is contagious'

3. Be a team player

You won't make it through training alone; you'll need help from fellow cadets, friends and colleagues.

4. Practise the art of presentation

Learn how to make hospital corners on your bed and master the art of "smiley socks", shoe polishing and ironing. If you can't do the little things right, you'll never do the big things right.

5. Accept you'll get things wrong

No matter how hard you try to get everything perfect, sometimes you'll get things wrong; don't dwell on it, move on. The purpose of the training is to see how you perform when you fail.

6. Be brave

Try new things and work hard to be the best you can. Then think about how to be better.

7. Set the standard

The standard you walk past is the standard you accept. There will be cheats, cowards and bullies in the world – challenge them.

8. Be your best in the darkest moments

When everything goes wrong or seems utterly chaotic, remain calm and composed. Trust in yourself and what you have learnt: your tactical skills, physical strength and mental resilience. Be clear and make a decision.

9. Keep your sense of humour

When you're cold, wet, hungry and still have another 30km to go with a full pack on your back, make a joke, sing, laugh ... and it will get better. The power of hope is contagious.

10. Never give up

Remember the saying: 'winners never quit – and quitters never win'. Accept the pressures of training: the runs, the obstacle courses, the drill and the rules. Be determined and you could achieve the ultimate prize: a commission from the greatest military academy in the world.

OFFICER CADET
JARGON 101

Do you know the difference between being bluerz and redderz? **OCdt Callum Nickless** of RMAS gives the lowdown on the lingo.

'Clip: struggling to meet the demands of the task at hand'

© RMAS

To Inspire To Achieve

Officer cadets march past the front of Royal Military Academy Sandhurst

© Crown copyright

Bluerz *(see Redderz)*
Not running fast enough or not carrying enough kit, and therefore feeling cold.

Buckshee
Easy.

Chip shop
Anything sub-par.

Clip/being in clip
Struggling to meet the demands of the task at hand.

Hanging out
Failure to prepare thoroughly fitness-wise, and therefore paying the consequences.

Jack
Not pulling your weight for your teammates – and, by far, the worst thing ever.

Pop smoke
Some call this retreating, but as the British Army never retreats, it's better referred to as "tactical withdrawal".

Rats
Disgusting or gross (also *gipping, gopping, honking* and *howling*).

Redderz *(see Bluerz)*
Red in the face; flustered after too much running around in too much kit.

Rupert
A newly commissioned officer who fits the old-fashioned stereotype of a British Army officer.

Generally speaking, they are academically competent but find everyday tasks a struggle – be it reading a map or even being able to adequately take care of their own hygiene. On meeting their soldiers for the first time, the scene is synonymous with feeding a lamb to a pack of hyenas.

Scoff
Food (also *scran*).

Scoffhouse
Dining facility for the production and dissemination of scoff.

Snapped
A more extreme version of *threaders* i.e., when you have passed the point of no return.

Squaddies
The soldiers of the British Army are the bread and butter of the organisation, and are great and noble kin. Plus, they usually know more about an officer's job than the officer does.

Threaders
How CSM feels when one of the new platoon commanders makes a boo-boo on a Friday afternoon (AKA "extremely cheesed off").

2020 Army Cadets QUIZ

50 tricky questions to find out just how good your Army Cadets knowledge is, and whether you've been paying attention this year...

ATTENTION!

Just how carefully have you been reading the book?

1) Who became National Honorary Colonel of Army Cadets in November 2019?

2) What should you do if a crocodile has your leg in its mouth?

3) On an OS map, what do the numbers on the contour lines tell you?

4) Who founded an Army Cadet unit for young workers at the London Stock Exchange?

5) Which five survival skills does Phil Campion believe every cadet should master?

6) What's the one piece of kit General David Eastman says he couldn't live without?

7) Which former Royal Marines commando smashed two world records by rowing across the Atlantic from mainland Europe to South America?

8) What's the RMAS jargon used to describe someone red in the face from running around in too much kit?

9) Which Guinness World Records™ attempt did Sally Orange and Jordan Wylie undertake in October 2020?

10) Army Cadets has its own limited-edition version of which classic board game?

LIFE IN LOCKDOWN

Monumental moments and unusual activities in 2020

11) On which date did the UK's nationwide lockdown begin?

12) Which online video chat service jumped from 10m to 300m daily users between December 2019 and April 2020?

13) British grocers saw a 92 per cent increase in sales of which foodstuff in the four weeks leading up to 22 March?

14) Restaurants sold more than 100 million meals as part of which government scheme?

15) On which day of the week did the nation come together to clap for carers?

Army Cadets knowledge

How much do you know?

16) What is the Army Cadets motto?

17) What is the name of the project that aims to prevent and remove discrimination within the ACF?

18) Which social reformer formed London's first independent Cadet Battalion (a concept that became the Army Cadet Force) in 1889?

19) In which year did female cadets first join the ACF?

20) What star level must you reach to become a cadet staff sergeant?

21) How old must you be to become a CFAV?

22) When performing drill, on the command 'quick march' which foot do you step with?

23) The ACF is one of four cadet organisations – name the other three.

24) In 2010, the Cadet movement celebrated which anniversary?

25) What does CCAT stand for?

26) Who is Army Cadets' Commander Cadets?

27) What is the highest star level a cadet can achieve?

28) What does RFCA stand for?

29) Should the cap badge on your beret be above your left or right eye?

30) What's the earliest age you could become a cadet?

2020 Army Cadets QUIZ

Month by month

Hint: you'll need to scour the monthly round-ups to get these.

31) We pulled an April Fools' Day prank suggesting cadets would encounter something unusual during fieldcraft exercises. What was it?

32) The fourth annual STEM camp took place on Salisbury Plain during which month in 2019?

33) A group of cadet and CFAV drummers performed with which *Britain's Got Talent* winner in December 2019?

34) In December 2019, RSM Lily Andrews became one of 30 individuals to be awarded with which prestigious coin?

35) Where did the first ever Army Cadet Force Annual Conference take place in January 2020?

36) How many CFAVs discovered they had been granted state honours by Her Majesty The Queen in December 2019?

37) In which month during lockdown was the first Army Cadet digi-mag launched?

38) Cadets joined forces (virtually) in May to celebrate the 75th anniversary of which momentous event?

39) A message from Her Majesty The Queen marked the virtual celebrations of which annual event in June?

40) Which Army Cadet building was lit in the colours of the rainbow to mark Pride Month?

41) A courageous group of cadets used their first aid skills to help an elderly man in July. Which detachment were they from?

42) In March 2020, ex-cadet Sam Zarych used his technical skills to help build and deliver new CPAP breathing machines. To which Formula One HPP Team is Sam apprenticed?

43) Which award did CFAV Scott Baker receive as a result of undertaking heroic first-aid actions in August?

44) To which role was Brigadier Stuart Williams appointed in September 2020?

45) Ambassador Jordan Wylie, Champion Phil Campion and Captain Alison Campbell shared a series of personal audio messages with cadets via social media to mark which event in May?

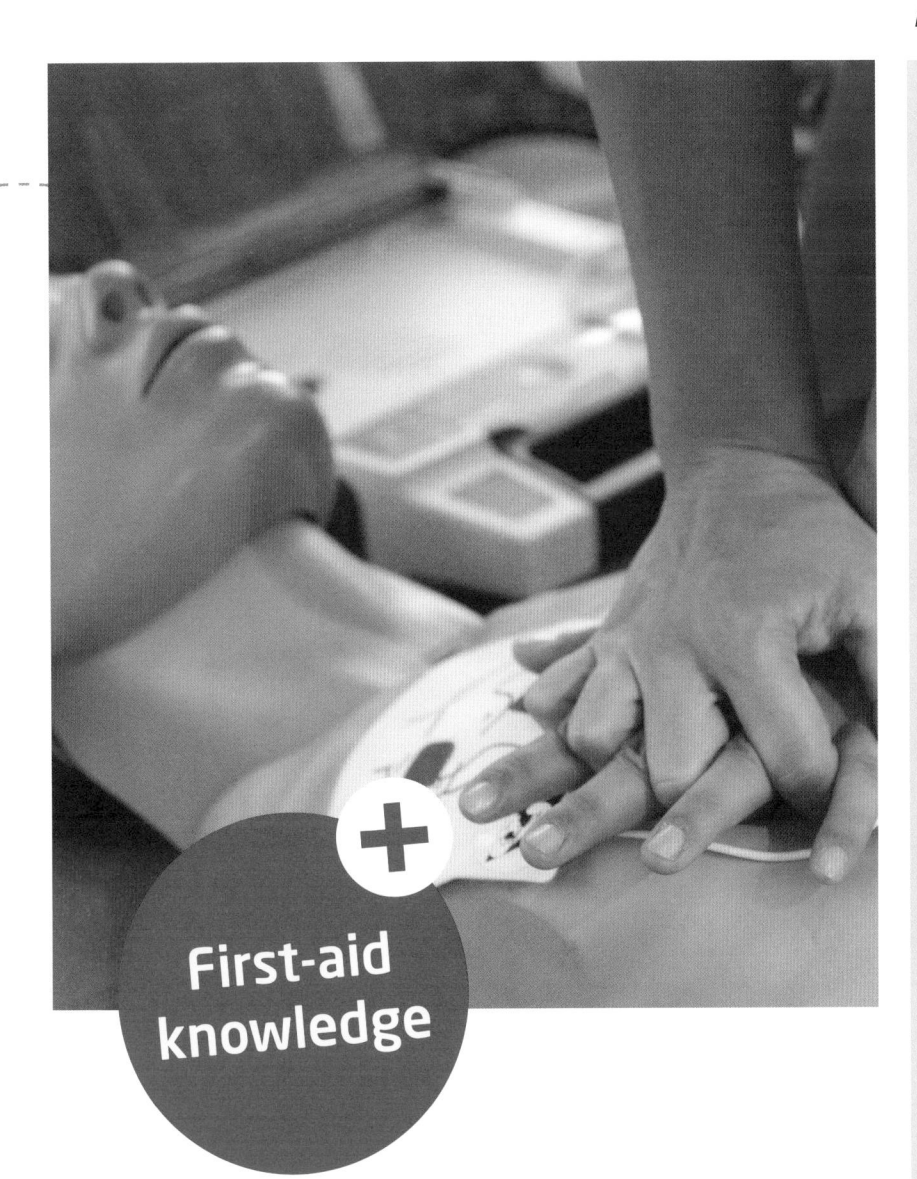

First-aid knowledge

Confident you know these basics?

46) How do you open the airways of an unconscious adult?

47) What rate of chest compressions should you aim for when administering CPR?

48) What drug can be offered to a victim suffering a suspected heart attack?

49) What does CPR stand for?

50) The FAST test helps to spot the symptoms of a stroke – what does it stand for?

Quiz

ANSWERS

» Attention!

1. Lorraine Kelly
2. Stick a thumb or finger in its eye
3. How high above sea level it is
4. Major Max Karo
5. Food and water, signalling, first aid, shelter and fire
6. Asics trainers
7. Aldo Kane
8. Redderz
9. Deepest Underground Marathon Distance Run (team)
10. Monopoly

» Life in lockdown

11. 23 March
12. Zoom
13. Flour
14. Eat Out To Help Out
15. Thursday

» Army Cadets knowledge

16. To Inspire To Achieve
17. ACF Step Change Diversity and Inclusion Project
18. Octavia Hill
19. 1979
20. APC 4 star
21. 18
22. Left
23. Combined Cadet Force, Sea Cadet Corps and Air Training Corps
24. 150th
25. Cadet Centre for Adventurous Training
26. Major General David Eastman MBE
27. Master Cadet
28. Reserve Forces' and Cadets' Association
29. Left
30. 12

» Month by month

31. Mobile refreshment van
32. October 2019
33. Colin Thackery
34. The Conductors' Coin
35. Royal Military Academy Sandhurst
36. Six
37. April
38. VE Day
39. Armed Forces Day
40. CTC Frimley Park
41. ACF Merseyside
42. Mercedes
43. Meritorious First Aid Award
44. Deputy Commander Cadets
45. Mental Health Awareness Week

» First-aid knowledge

46. Tilt the head back and lift the chin
47. 100-120 a minute
48. Aspirin
49. Cardiopulmonary resuscitation
50. Face, arms, speech, time

Army Cadet Yearbook Issue 1

203

Cadet Forces
MEDALS

The Cadet Forces Medal is awarded to recognise long and efficient service by commissioned officers and non-commissioned adult instructors of the UK Cadet Forces. Clasps are issued for every six additional years. Huge congratulations to everyone included in this October 2019 to September 2020 collation.

6TH CLASP

MAJ	S J	**SCULL**	ACF	City and County of Bristol ACF

5TH CLASP

CAPT	S	**BROOKS**	ACF	Gloucestershire ACF
MAJ	G L	**MARTIN**	ACF	Dyfed and Glamorgan ACF
CAPT	M C J	**PRICE**	ACF	Gwent and Powys ACF
MAJ	D J	**SAUNDERS**	ACF	Gwent and Powys ACF
CAPT	R S	**WALLEN**	ACF	City of London and NE Sector ACF

4TH CLASP

SMI	A F	**HAMILTON**	ACF	City and County of Bristol ACF
CAPT	S O	**SPILSBURY**	ACF	ACF HQ, Kent
SMI	R	**ALDCROFT**	ACF	Northumbria ACF
SMI	P	**CHISWELL**	ACF	Leicestershire, Northamptonshire and Rutland ACF
CAPT	V J	**BURRELL-TAYLOR MBE**	CCF	Charterhouse School CCF, Surrey
MAJ	M D	**SMALL**	ACF	The Royal County of Berkshire ACF
SSI	G J	**TENNANT**	ACF	Northumbria ACF
SMI	A P	**WOOLEY**	ACF	Middlesex and North West London ACF
MAJ	J	**REYNOLDS**	ACF	Glasgow and Lanarkshire Bn ACF
CAPT	R J	**WALLEN**	ACF	Buckinghamshire ACF
LT	P J	**FARMER**	ACF	Hampshire and Isle of Wight ACF
LT COL	H	**CANAVAN**	ACF	Argyll and Sutherland Highlanders Bn ACF
COL	M	**KNIGHT MBE**	ACF	Cambridgeshire ACF
MAJ	J L	**DANIELS**	ACF	Northumbria ACF
SSI	R	**HUGHES**	ACF	Argyll and Sutherland Highlanders Bn ACF
LT	A D	**FULLER**	ACF	Kent ACF
SMI	N	**WOLLISTON**	ACF	Greater London South East Sector ACF

3RD CLASP

MAJ	C J	**CHERRY**	CCF	Colfe's School CCF
MAJ	A J	**PRICE**	ACF	Staffordshire and West Midlands (NS) ACF
SSI	R	**ANNIS**	ACF	Cambridgeshire ACF
MAJ	G	**MACDONALD**	ACF	1st Bn The Highlanders ACF
SMI	M J	**PROWSE**	ACF	Wiltshire ACF
CAPT	C F	**CARMICHAEL**	CCF	Dean Close School, Gloucestershire
SMI	T M	**JACKSON**	ACF	Dorset ACF
LT COL	A R	**GARRETT**	ACF	Dorset ACF
CAPT	M	**ROACH**	ACF	Argyll and Sutherland Highlanders Bn ACF
MAJ	J	**REYNOLDS**	ACF	Glasgow and Lanarkshire Bn ACF
SSI	T A	**CALDECOAT**	ACF	Bedfordshire and Hertfordshire ACF
RSMI	J M	**INGLE**	ACF	Leicestershire, Northamptonshire and Rutland ACF
CAPT	K	**FISHER**	ACF	Yorkshire (N and W) ACF
SMI	R A	**GODWIN-JONES**	ACF	Staffordshire and West Midlands (NS) ACF
SSI	D L	**SULLIVAN**	ACF	Leicestershire, Northamptonshire and Rutland ACF
SSI	W	**PALMER**	ACF	Leicestershire, Northamptonshire and Rutland ACF
SMI	J D	**ROGERS**	ACF	Leicestershire, Northamptonshire and Rutland ACF
COL	P L	**SAUNDERS**	ACF	Gloucestershire ACF
CAPT	D J	**RUTHERFORD**	ACF	1st (Northern Ireland) Bn ACF
LT COL	D J K	**TUCKER**	ACF	Warwickshire and West Midlands (South Sector) ACF
COL	T M	**FARMER**	ACF	Hampshire and Isle of Wight ACF
LT COL	M Z	**HAMID**	CCF	Erskine Stewart's Melville School, Edinburgh
MAJ	R C L	**MACDONALD**	ACF	Greater Manchester ACF

2ND CLASP

SMI	S	**MORROW**	ACF	Cambridgeshire ACF
SSI	P A	**COX**	ACF	Bedfordshire and Hertfordshire ACF
MAJ	D	**ELIE**	ACF	Clwyd and Gwynedd ACF
MAJ	M L	**CRAVEN**	ACF	Clwyd and Gwynedd ACF
LT COL	A J	**LESTER**	ACF	Staffordshire and West Midlands (NS) ACF
MAJ	J	**BEAKE**	ACF	City and County of Bristol ACF
SMI	P L	**HICKERMAN**	ACF	Derbyshire ACF (Mercian)
MAJ	C L	**REID**	CCF	Cheltenham College CCF, Gloucestershire
CAPT	F J	**SIMKINS**	CCF	Hurstpierpoint College CCF, West Sussex
CAPT	H V	**RICHARDSON**	CCF	Woodbridge School CCF, Suffolk
LT COL	P D	**TOOZE**	ACF	City and County of Bristol ACF
MAJ	S R	**FLANAGAN**	ACF	Humberside and South Yorkshire ACF
CAPT	M A	**CALAZ**	ACF	Wiltshire ACF
LT	E L	**MATTHEWS**	ACF	Yorkshire (N and W) ACF
LT COL	P C	**DEAKIN**	ACF	Cornwall ACF
CAPT	Z L	**WAKE**	ACF	Hampshire and Isle of Wight ACF
LT COL	S A	**NICHOLSON**	ACF	Devon ACF
LT	D C	**SQUIRE**	ACF	Devon ACF
SSI	M E	**HOLLAND**	ACF	Devon ACF
MAJ	D J	**BUCKLEY**	ACF	Humberside and South Yorkshire ACF
CAPT	J	**REYNOLDS**	ACF	Glasgow and Lanarkshire Bn ACF
MAJ	R	**MAXWELL**	ACF	Clwyd and Gwynedd ACF
MAJ	R	**MURRAY**	ACF	NAL Cadet Branch HQ Regional Comd, Hampshire
LT COL	G M	**SMITH**	ACF	Angus and Dundee Bn ACF
MAJ	P	**THORNLEY**	ACF	Durham ACF
SMI	S J	**CAIRNS**	ACF	Essex ACF
SMI	S J	**WALKER**	ACF	Essex ACF
MAJ	J F L	**GAIGER**	ACF	Essex ACF
SMI	L M	**GROOM**	ACF	Bedfordshire and Hertfordshire ACF
LT	T W	**CHAPPELL**	ACF	Leicestershire, Northamptonshire and Rutland ACF
SMI	K J	**CROSS**	ACF	Derbyshire ACF
SMI	Z	**AUNG**	ACF	City of London and NE Sector ACF
MAJ	J M	**ROBINSON**	ACF	City of London and NE Sector ACF
SMI	F P	**NICOL**	ACF	Angus and Dundee Bn ACF
MAJ	N	**PATTON**	ACF	Yorkshire (N and W) ACF
SMI	G	**EDWARDS**	ACF	Staffordshire and West Midlands (NS) ACF
SMI	B C	**SNOWDEN**	ACF	Devon ACF
MAJ	P L	**CLARKE**	ACF	Devon ACF
SMI	I	**COLLEY**	ACF	The Royal County of Berkshire ACF
MAJ	D J	**ANSTEY**	ACF	City and County of Bristol ACF
MAJ	M J	**LEHMAN**	ACF	Kent ACF
SMI	S E	**WHITWORTH**	ACF	Cambridgeshire ACF
SMI	D P	**ECCLES**	ACF	Lancashire ACF

MAJ	K W	**JOBSON**	ACF	Northumbria ACF
SSI	L E	**GILCHRIST**	ACF	Northumbria ACF
SMI	I H	**BROWN**	ACF	Northumbria ACF
LT COL	A T	**SMITH**	ACF	Suffolk ACF
SSI	M R	**FULCHER**	ACF	Greater London South East Sector ACF
SMI	R G	**KIRKLAND**	ACF	Buckinghamshire ACF
MAJ	D J F	**KONSTANTINIOUS**	ACF	Greater London South East Sector ACF
SSI	J	**ROBINSON**	ACF	Northumbria ACF
COL	D J F	**SMITH**	ACF	Greater London South East Sector ACF
MAJ	M B	**SPENCE**	ACF	Northumbria ACF
CAPT	A W	**WOODS**	ACF	Northumbria ACF

1ST CLASP

CAPT	R	**WATHEY**	ACF	Yorkshire (N and W) ACF
WO1	K J	**STOLLERY**	CCF	Woodbridge School CCF
CAPT	L V	**RICKARD**	CCF	Woodbridge School CCF
MAJ	G E	**HUGHES**	ACF	Clwyd and Gwynedd ACF
LT	J M K	**MURRIN**	CCF	Exeter School CCF, Devon
CHPLN(CF3)	S F	**CADDY**	ACF	Lancashire ACF
SMI	H	**GOOD**	ACF	City of London and NE Sector ACF
MAJ	C L	**REID**	CCF	Cheltenham College CCF, Gloucestershire
CAPT	F J	**SIMKINS**	CCF	Hurstpierpoint College CCF, West Sussex
SSI	N	**SCOTT**	ACF	2nd Bn The Highlanders ACF
2LT	K	**STARK**	ACF	Black Watch Bn ACF, Perthshire
CAPT	C A	**JOHNSON**	CCF	Ash Manor School CCF, Surrey
CAPT	L T	**DYNAN**	ACF	Oxfordshire ACF
SMI	R K	**WILKINS**	ACF	Oxfordshire ACF
CAPT	A	**AIDONIS**	CCF	Charterhouse School CCF, Surrey
CAPT	N	**ASHLEE-McCRAE**	CCF	Hockerill Anglo-European College, Hertfordshire
SSI	S J	**GOODING**	ACF	Lincolnshire ACF
CAPT	B E N	**JAMES**	ACF	Buckinghamshire ACF
CAPT	K D	**JARDINE**	ACF	Cumbria ACF
SSI	G S	**LIGHT**	ACF	Hampshire and Isle of Wight ACF
SI	S S	**MEDWAY**	ACF	Hampshire and Isle of Wight ACF
SMI	P A	**QUINN**	ACF	Greater Manchester ACF
RSMI	B J	**TARGETT**	ACF	Buckinghamshire ACF
MAJ	N C	**WATSON**	ACF	Lincolnshire ACF
SSI	N	**MACHIN**	ACF	Leicestershire, Northamptonshire and Rutland ACF
MAJ	G	**COOK**	ACF	Oxfordshire (The Rifles) Bn ACF
MAJ	J R	**STOREY**	CCF	Downside School CCF, Somerset
LT	S C	**PALMA**	CCF	Warminster School, Wiltshire
LT COL	M	**CLARKE**	ACF	Dyfed and Glamorgan ACF
CAPT	H E	**STARK**	ACF	Dyfed and Glamorgan ACF
SMI	C E	**MAXWELL**	ACF	1st (Northern Ireland) Bn ACF
RSMI	O C A	**WELLS**	ACF	Dorset ACF
SSI	A	**SMITH**	ACF	Nottinghamshire ACF
CAPT	S	**RIDING**	ACF	Greater Manchester ACF
CAPT	Z L	**WAKE**	ACF	Hampshire and Isle of Wight ACF
SSI	J J	**McPARLAND**	ACF	2nd Northern Ireland Bn ACF, Belfast
CAPT	A	**CAMPBELL**	ACF	2nd Northern Ireland Bn ACF, Belfast
SSI	I W	**McCLEARY**	CCF	Highfield Leadership Academy CCF, Lancashire
SMI	T	**TRAYNOR**	ACF	Glasgow and Lanarkshire Bn ACF
CAPT	J	**REYNOLDS**	ACF	Glasgow and Lanarkshire Bn ACF
MAJ	D G	**FLOWER**	ACF	Dorset ACF
SMI	P E	**REMNANT**	ACF	Hampshire and Isle of Wight ACF
SMI	A I	**CLARK**	CCF	Monkton Combe School, Somerset
SSI	F J	**GILKES**	ACF	Leicestershire, Northamptonshire and Rutland ACF
SSI	J A	**WARD**	ACF	Derbyshire ACF
MAJ	W	**RATHJE-MORRIS**	ACF	Kent ACF
CAPT	C D	**NORMAN MBE**	ACF	Hampshire and Isle of Wight ACF
MAJ	J H	**HUGHES**	CCF	Clifton College CCF, Bristol
SSI	G A	**MITCHELL**	ACF	Yorkshire (N and W) ACF
REV(CF3)	A P	**JEANS**	ACF	Wiltshire ACF
SSI	A J	**KEYLOCK**	CCF	St Edwards School CCF, Gloucestershire
MAJ	M	**GRIFFITHS**	ACF	Gloucestershire ACF
CAPT	M V	**JOHN**	ACF	Gloucestershire ACF
MAJ	A C	**BRADY**	ACF	Gloucestershire ACF
CAPT	L J	**CORNER**	ACF	Devon ACF
MAJ	J L	**MOORE**	ACF	1st (Northern Ireland) Bn ACF

To Inspire To Achieve

MAJ	D D	EVANS	CCF	Dean Close School, Gloucestershire
SMI	I	COLLEY	ACF	The Royal County of Berkshire ACF
SMI	P G	CLARK	ACF	Bedfordshire and Hertfordshire ACF
CAPT	Z M	LUKE	ACF	Northumbria ACF
CAPT	S	AIR	ACF	Northumbria ACF
CAPT	P J	LAWRENCE	ACF	Northumbria ACF
SMI	L	CONROY	ACF	Argyll and Sutherland Highlanders Bn ACF
CAPT	C S	DEANS	ACF	Argyll and Sutherland Highlanders Bn ACF
MAJ	J D	MONEY	CCF	Cranleigh School, Surrey
SMI	T M	ALLEN	ACF	Cornwall ACF
SMI	M Q	CLARKE	ACF	Greater London South East Sector ACF
CAPT	K	DENT	ACF	Northumbria ACF
LT COL	S	JOHNSON	ACF	Greater London South East Sector ACF
SSI	R A	MORRIS	ACF	Cornwall ACF
2LT	M B	O'SULLIVAN	ACF	Greater London South East Sector ACF
SI	A	OXBOROUGH	ACF	Northumbria ACF
MAJ	A A	PUGH	ACF	Northumbria ACF
RSMI	F A	QUINN	CCF	Reading School CCF, Berkshire
SSI	J	ROBINSON	ACF	Northumbria ACF
SI	L A	SIMPSON	ACF	Northumbria ACF
MAJ	M B	SPENCE	ACF	Northumbria ACF
SSI	S P	STADEN	ACF	Greater London South East Sector ACF
CAPT	A W	WOODS	ACF	Northumbria ACF

CADET FORCES MEDAL

CAPT	S G	PAYNE	ACF	Suffolk ACF
SSI	P	MURROW	ACF	Suffolk ACF
SSI	T	HAZELDINE	ACF	Suffolk ACF
SSI	G	DAVIES	ACF	Gwent and Powys ACF
LT	D	NUTBEAM	ACF	Hampshire and Isle of Wight ACF
SSI	S M	BROADHEAD	ACF	Humberside and South Yorkshire ACF
SMI	K	BESSELL	ACF	Middlesex and North West London ACF
SI	N L	KAY	ACF	Middlesex and North West London ACF
SMI	T R	LINDSAY	ACF	Middlesex and North West London ACF
CAPT	T C G	MARTIN	ACF	1st Bn The Highlanders ACF
SMI	E	MILLS	ACF	1st Bn The Highlanders ACF
CAPT	S F	REVELL	ACF	Suffolk ACF
CAPT	D C	SHOOTER	CCF	Welbeck DSFC
LT	A C	ELLIOT	ACF	Clwyd and Gwynedd ACF
CAPT	A D	CARR	ACF	City and County of Bristol ACF
SSI	N	MITCHAM	ACF	Cambridgeshire ACF
LT	J M K	PEGG	CCF	Exeter School CCF, Devon
LT	D	STONE	ACF	Gloucestershire ACF
SSI	D E	GRAHAM-YOUNG	ACF	West Lowland Bn ACF
SSI	M D	BROOKSBANK	ACF	Staffordshire and West Midlands (NS) ACF
LT	B I	PERCIVAL	CCF	St Brigid's School CCF, Denbighshire
MAJ	S M	FRILING	CCF	Cheltenham College CCF, Gloucestershire
MAJ	R J	PENNY	CCF	Cheltenham College CCF, Gloucestershire
MAJ	J F	WIGGELL MBE	CCF	Dover Grammar School for Boys, Kent
SSI	S	TAYLOR	ACF	Black Watch Bn ACF
SI	G	GDANIEC	ACF	Nottinghamshire ACF
CAPT	J	DARROCH BEM	ACF	Cheshire ACF
SSI	R	DEVLIN	ACF	2nd Bn The Highlanders ACF
SSI	M	GOATCHER	CCF	City of London Academy (HAC) CCF, London
SSI	K A	GRIMSEY	ACF	Hampshire and Isle of Wight ACF
CAPT	S J	JEPHCOTE	CCF	City of London Academy (HAC) CCF, London
CAPT	F C L	SHORT	ACF	Greater Manchester ACF
SSI	M L	BRUNNOCK	ACF	Gwent and Powys ACF
CAPT	P A	HARRIS	ACF	Gwent and Powys ACF
SSI	R T	DODGE	ACF	Leicestershire, Northamptonshire and Rutland ACF
CAPT	G A	McDOOL	ACF	Humberside and South Yorkshire ACF
CAPT	C M	KIRK	ACF	Humberside and South Yorkshire ACF
CAPT	A W	WIGGINS	ACF	Wiltshire ACF
LT	D J	BULL	ACF	Somerset Cadet Bn (The Rifles) ACF
SMI	D L	ANDREWS	ACF	HQ Devon ACF
SMI	E L	SAUNDERS	ACF	Gwent and Powys ACF
SI	E L	ANDERSON	ACF	Cleveland ACF
SI	M J	NEWMAN	ACF	Cleveland ACF
CAPT	D M	HOPPER	ACF	Cleveland ACF

MAJ	S L	**WATSON**	ACF	Cleveland ACF
SI	R J	**BENNETT**	ACF	Cleveland ACF
SSI	A D J	**HURCUMB**	ACF	HQ South West London ACF
LT	C J	**LINE**	ACF	HQ South West London ACF
MAJ	K D W	**CROWE**	ACF	1st (Northern Ireland) Bn ACF
LT	B N	**MOORE**	ACF	Kent ACF
SMI	D	**GALLAGHER**	ACF	Buckinghamshire ACF
SMI	T M	**YOUNG**	ACF	Buckinghamshire ACF
LT	S L	**HOLMES**	CCF	Hele's School, Devon
LT	A J	**GEORGE**	CCF	Dean Close School, Gloucestershire
SSI	R J	**JOBSON**	ACF	Northumbria ACF
SSI	G K A	**MILLER**	ACF	Lincolnshire ACF
SMI	P E	**THOMAS**	ACF	Dorset ACF
CAPT	D	**BROOKS**	ACF	Dorset ACF
SSI	K	**JOYNES**	ACF	Dorset ACF
LT	C J	**RONDEL**	ACF	Dorset ACF
REV(CF3)	G	**FIELDHOUSE-BYRNE**	ACF	Greater Manchester ACF
SSI	A	**ROBINSON**	ACF	Leicestershire, Northamptonshire and Rutland ACF
CAPT	A	**EMERY**	ACF	Wiltshire ACF
SMI	J	**KNOWLES**	ACF	Wiltshire ACF
SMI	R G	**RUTHERFORD**	ACF	Dorset ACF
LT	J E	**PRIOR**	ACF	Essex ACF
SMI	L	**FLANAGAN**	ACF	Merseyside ACF
RSMI	J L	**CARMICHAEL**	ACF	Merseyside ACF
SMI	K G	**ANDREWS**	ACF	Merseyside ACF
SMI	J W	**LIGHT**	ACF	Cornwall ACF
RSMI	L M	**HEALY**	CCF	Radley College CCF, Oxfordshire
LT	J G	**GUNNILL**	CCF	Gad's Hill School CCF, Kent
MAJ	S E	**DRAIN**	ACF	Hampshire and Isle of Wight ACF
SMI	P J	**EASTLEY**	ACF	Devon ACF
SSI	T R	**BEST**	ACF	Gloucestershire ACF
LT	A M	**BARRACLOUGH**	ACF	Gloucestershire ACF
SMI	R D	**McNEILL**	ACF	Glasgow and Lanarkshire Bn ACF
SSI	N	**ASHLEY**	ACF	Wiltshire ACF
SI	D J	**HARRISON**	ACF	Humberside and South Yorkshire ACF
CAPT	J	**REYNOLDS**	ACF	Glasgow and Lanarkshire Bn ACF
SI	P E	**REMNANT**	ACF	Hampshire and Isle of Wight ACF
CAPT	P T	**ANDERTON**	ACF	Greater Manchester ACF
SSI	J C	**BASHIR**	ACF	Greater Manchester ACF
SSI	S	**BLACK**	ACF	West Lowland Bn ACF Ayrshire
SSI	I G	**CAMPBELL**	ACF	Lancashire ACF
COL	J M	**COIA**	ACF	Cadet Branch HQ SW ACF, Wiltshire
CAPT	M J L	**COMMANDER**	CCF	Benenden School CCF, Kent
MAJ	M A	**DOYLE**	ACF	NAL Cadet Branch HQ Regional Comd, Hampshire
SSI	M E	**GRAY**	ACF	HQ South West London Sector ACF
LT	J W	**JOHNSON**	CCF	St James Boys' School CCF, Surrey
CAPT	G M	**KIFF**	CCF	Brentwood School CCF, Essex
SI	Y K	**LINE**	ACF	HQ South West London Sector ACF
LT	A C E	**NORTH**	CCF	Caterham School CCF, Surrey
LT	S	**PERVIN**	CCF	Welbeck DSFC, Leicestershire
COL	L C A	**RANSON**	ACF	NAL Cadet Branch HQ Regional Comd, Hampshire
CAPT	V	**SQUIRES**	ACF	Devon ACF
MAJ	K R	**WALTERS**	ACF	NAL Cadet Branch HQ Regional Comd, Hampshire
SMI	L J	**EVANS**	ACF	Essex ACF
SSI	M	**BRUNETTI**	ACF	Bedfordshire and Hertfordshire ACF
SSI	P L	**MABBOTT**	ACF	Leicestershire, Northamptonshire and Rutland ACF
CAPT	H L	**LAMMING**	ACF	Lincolnshire ACF
SSI	D L	**BRAMMER**	ACF	Lincolnshire ACF
LT	P G	**BOUCHER**	ACF	Lincolnshire ACF
MAJ	E L	**BURTENSHAW**	ACF	South West London Sector ACF
CAPT	G S	**DU-TRACY**	ACF	Dorset ACF
RSMI	A W	**STOCK**	ACF	City of London and NE Sector ACF
RSMI	P L	**NUTLEY**	ACF	Northumbria ACF
SSI	M A	**KNOX**	ACF	Cumbria ACF
SMI	K J	**URQUHART**	ACF	Angus and Dundee Bn ACF
SI	A A	**BECKMAN**	ACF	Leicestershire, Northamptonshire and Rutland ACF
SSI	N J	**WALTHAM**	ACF	Nottinghamshire ACF

To Inspire To Achieve

SI	E M	**MANUEL**	ACF	Shropshire ACF
SMI	J Z	**HAYDEN**	ACF	Shropshire ACF
SI	M	**BERESFORD**	ACF	Yorkshire (N and W) ACF
SSI	A M	**THIRKILL**	ACF	Yorkshire (N and W) ACF
LT	C	**MASSEY**	ACF	Yorkshire (N and W) ACF
SMI	W P	**DUGMORE**	ACF	Staffordshire and West Midlands (NS) ACF
MAJ	J A	**PEPLOW**	ACF	Leicestershire, Northamptonshire and Rutland ACF
RSMI	C M	**BARNES**	ACF	Wiltshire ACF
LT	P M	**GLADWIN**	ACF	Leicestershire, Northamptonshire and Rutland ACF
CAPT	M J D	**FELLOWS**	ACF	Gloucestershire ACF
CAPT	C S I	**ANGUS**	ACF	Somerset Cadet Bn (The Rifles) ACF
SMI	K W	**BOON**	ACF	Devon ACF
SMI	W M	**PATON**	ACF	Devon ACF
LT	G M	**LANCEY**	ACF	Somerset ACF
LT	P M	**ANDERSON**	ACF	City of London and NE Sector ACF
SMI	D G	**ROBERTSON**	ACF	Clwyd and Gwynedd ACF
SSI	R A	**SHARPE**	ACF	Surrey ACF
SMI	H	**WATERWORTH**	ACF	Sussex ACF
SSI	S L	**McPHERSON**	ACF	Yorkshire (N and W) ACF
SMI	P J	**COWARD**	ACF	Somerset Cadet Bn (The Rifles) ACF
SMI	J S	**UPWOOD**	ACF	Bedfordshire and Hertfordshire ACF
CAPT	C E S	**CALLENDER**	ACF	Bedfordshire and Hertfordshire ACF
LT	D	**YOUNG**	ACF	Essex ACF
SSI	D L	**SMITH**	ACF	Lincolnshire ACF
CAPT	R A J	**FROST**	ACF	Devon ACF
SMI	N C	**FAWSITT**	ACF	Essex ACF
CAPT	M	**COOPER**	ACF	Essex ACF
LT	D G	**SMALLEY**	ACF	Lancashire ACF
SI	J C	**PORTER**	ACF	Lancashire ACF
SSI	M A	**D'ANDREA**	ACF	Lancashire ACF
MAJ	G D	**WATSON**	ACF	Northumbria ACF
CAPT	D M	**COLE**	ACF	Northumbria ACF
LT	S G	**WATSON**	ACF	Northumbria ACF
SMI	C P	**SHEEHAN**	ACF	Suffolk ACF
LT	P D	**MILDREN**	ACF	Suffolk ACF
CAPT	A H	**SHAIKH**	ACF	Warwickshire and West Midlands (South Sector) ACF
SSI	A	**COOK**	ACF	Warwickshire and West Midlands (South Sector) ACF
SI	J C	**GREAVES**	ACF	Warwickshire and West Midlands (South Sector) ACF
SI	A R	**MORRIS**	ACF	Warwickshire and West Midlands (South Sector) ACF
RSMI	F	**BYRNE**	CCF	Shrewsbury School CCF, Shropshire
SMI	N	**MURPHY**	ACF	Argyll and Sutherland Highlanders Bn ACF
SMI	A	**MULHOLLAND**	ACF	Argyll and Sutherland Highlanders Bn ACF
SSI	S D	**ALMOND**	ACF	Leicestershire, Northamptonshire and Rutland ACF
SI	K	**FORD**	ACF	Leicestershire, Northamptonshire and Rutland ACF
LT	S J	**HAWKINS**	CCF	Judd School, Kent
CAPT	C A	**SAN JOSE**	CCF	Radley College, Oxfordshire
SMI	A	**MORLAND**	ACF	Wiltshire ACF
CAPT	V	**ACQUAH**	ACF	Greater London South East Sector ACF
RSMI	S	**AFSHAR**	ACF	Middlesex and North West London ACF
SI	R J	**BROWN**	ACF	Leicestershire, Northamptonshire and Rutland ACF
SMI	A H	**COX**	ACF	Devon ACF
SSI	J	**DAVIS**	ACF	Angus and Dundee Bn ACF
SMI	D W	**DUDGEON**	ACF	Northumbria ACF
SI	A C	**FERGUSON**	CCF	Reading School CCF, Berkshire
SSI	A P	**GAY**	CCF	Writhlington School CCF, Somerset
SSI	M R	**LOCKEY**	ACF	Greater London South East Sector ACF
SI	S T	**McMICHAEL**	ACF	1st (Northern Ireland) Bn ACF
SMI	P I	**MOONEY**	ACF	Merseyside ACF
SSI	C L	**MOVERLEY**	ACF	Humberside and South Yorkshire ACF
SMI	A A	**PUGH**	ACF	Northumbria ACF
SI	D	**ROBERTS**	ACF	Durham ACF
SSI	J	**ROBINSON**	ACF	Northumbria ACF
SI	L A	**SIMPSON**	ACF	Northumbria ACF
MAJ	D R	**SLATER**	ACF	Northumbria ACF
SSI	D A	**STARK**	ACF	Northumbria ACF
SSI	C L	**TELFORD**	ACF	Northumbria ACF
SMI	S R	**WALES**	ACF	Northumbria ACF